# Women under the Third Reich

# Women under the Third Reich

## A Biographical Dictionary

Shaaron Cosner and Victoria Cosner

Greenwood Press
Westport, Connecticut • London

**Library of Congress Cataloging-in-Publication Data**

Cosner, Shaaron.
    Women under the Third Reich : a biographical dictionary / by
Shaaron Cosner and Victoria Cosner.
        p.    cm.
    Includes bibliographical references and index.
    ISBN 0–313–30315–0 (alk. paper)
    1. National socialism and women—Dictionaries.  2. Women—Germany—
History—20th century—Dictionaries.  3. Fascism and women—
Germany—Dictionaries.  4. World War, 1939–1945—Prisoners and
prisons, German—Dictionaries.  5. World War, 1939–1945—Women—
Germany—Dictionaries.  I. Cosner, Victoria, 1965–  .  II. Title.
HQ1623.C65   1998
943.086'082—dc21         97–45641

British Library Cataloguing in Publication Data is available.

Library of Congress Catalog Card Number: 97–45641
ISBN: 0–313–30315–0

First published in 1998

Greenwood Press, 88 Post Road West, Westport, CT 06881
An imprint of Greenwood Publishing Group, Inc.

Printed in the United States of America

The paper used in this book complies with the
Permanent Paper Standard issued by the National
Information Standards Organization (Z39.48–1984).

10 9 8 7 6 5 4 3 2 1

**Copyright Acknowledgments**

Every reasonable effort has been made to trace the owners of copyright materials in this
book, but in some instances this has proven impossible. The author and publisher will
be glad to receive information leading to more complete acknowledgments in subsequent
printings of the book and in the meantime extend their apologies for any omissions.

This book is dedicated to all the women who we missed, or for whom, due to the vagaries of war and time, there are no records. Their stories deserve to be told.

# CONTENTS

# PREFACE

This work provides biographical and bibliographical portraits of approximately 100 women whose lives were affected by the Nazi regime. The story of World War II and the rise and fall of Adolf Hitler and the Third Reich has been primarily a story of men. The women who participated have been relegated largely to side notes. Yet women participated in all aspects of the war and on both sides of the Nazi flag. Women found the experience of the Third Reich just as exciting, just as profitable, and just as frightening as did men. Housewives smuggled documents, arms, and food in baskets, shopping bags, and baby carriages; they opened their homes to those fleeing the Third Reich despite the fact that, as Margaret Collins Weitz, in *Outwitting the Gestapo*, wrote, "a woman who sheltered or fed someone sought by the Gestapo—a political refugee, a Jew, an Allied aviator, or a resistant—risked death if caught . . . whereas the aviator would have been sent to a prisoner-of-war camp" (p. xiv).

Women worked side-by-side and roomed side-by-side in prisons and concentration camps, some with notable women of the period. Gemma Gluck, sister of New York Mayor Fiorello La Guardia, was held prisoner in Ravensbruck with Rose Tahelmann, wife of Ernst Tahelmann, the chief of the Communist Party in Germany. Josephine Ptacikova, an Austrian countess who used her castle and jewels to help save those fleeing the Reich (she died in the gas chamber after becoming blind from malnutrition); Countess Lilly de Raubuteau, a relative of the Danish Queen; the wife of the French Ambassador to Ankara, Madame Henry; Frau Wenzel, owner of fourteen estates in one of Germany's richest families (placed in Ravensbruck when she was 70 years old); the widow of the French Communist leader and writer Paul Valliant, Marie-Claude Valliant-Couturier; Genevieve de Gaulle, niece of Gen. Charles de Gualle; and Olga Himmler, sister of Gestapo chief Heinrich Himmler, imprisoned for having a love affair with a Polish officer in Warsaw, were all arrested and placed in prisons and concentration camps.

More than 827,000 Soviet women fought the onslaught of the Third Reich, 800,000 at the front as pilots, in tank crews, and with gun detachments and front-line medical personnel, and another 27,000 in partisan activities (Saywell, 1985, p. 131). In Russia, an estimated 2,700 women participated in partisan activities (p. 154). In Poland, women planned escape and supply routes through city sewers, smuggled weapons, joined assassination squads, and dealt in armed combat. Many of the fighters in the Warsaw Ghetto Uprising in 1943 were women and many fled into the forests, including one all-female regiment of 300 members (p. 102).

As Saywell also notes, escapees to England joined General Wladyslaw Sikorski and the Polish army supporters of the Allies to form a 6,700-member woman's auxiliary (p. 102). Forty thousand women were sworn in as members of the Home Army in Poland; 35,000 were trained in sabotage and weaponry (p. 102). About 10 percent of the Italian partisans were women who followed the historical precedents set during Italy's fight for independence in the nineteenth century and World War I (p. 74). In other countries women joined as agents in the SOE (Britain's Special Operations Executive), the BCRA (de Gaulle's Organization in France— the Bureau Central de Renseignements et d'Action) and many other resistance agencies. As a result, many were killed, tortured, imprisoned, and placed in concentration camps. There were more than 10,000 French women in Ravensbruck concentration camp, 85 percent for resistance activities, and all but 500 died (p. 34).

Despite the amazing accounts of bravery, despite the vast number of women who participated on both sides of the Third Reich, and despite their accomplishments, historians have often neglected them in the literature documenting the era. Researchers checking the index of a book on the Third Reich might see one or two names—usually Anne Frank and Eva Braun, occasionally Marlene Dietrich.

This book contains just a sampling of the women who played important roles in this terrifying period of world history. Although every woman who lived through the experience of the Third Reich should be

chronicled, choices for inclusion were based primarily on the availability
of material in the English language, and priority was given those women
whose autobiographies or biographies have been published. The choices
offer a diverse picture of personal character, treachery, and accomplishments, whether from wartime or occupational activities such as writers,
artists, filmmakers and film stars, musicians, and scientists. The authors
have attempted to include at least one woman from every part of the
intricate web that made up the occupied territories of the Third Reich,
representing a range of ages, occupations, nationalities, and political af-
filiations. Included are some who survived and some who did not, some
who died in obscurity, some who attained worldwide notoriety, and
others who simply disappeared without a trace.

It is hoped that *Women under the Third Reich* will offer an opportunity
to reclaim a small sampling of both the women who fought against and
the women who supported the Third Reich. It is also hoped that this
work will inspire other historians to research the work of women in
World War II.

Because the war was so chaotic and countries were constantly changing ownership, some towns, cities, or areas went through several name
changes. The authors attempted to use the name of each place as it was
known during most of the war. For example, Vilna was called Vilnius
after it was disputed between Poland and Lithuania following World
War I. However, in all sources used to research this book, it was referred
to as Vilna. In order to aid researchers in the future, Vilna was used
because that is the name they would research.

The same procedure was used for women's names. Because many of
the women who took part in the war were young and not married at
the time, they would have used their maiden name. Later, after they
married, many wrote about their experiences and became known by their
married names. Because their war activities were so prominent, research
often did not mention where or when the marriages took place. Again,
in order to aid researchers in the future, the authors have used the names
that these women used when they became prominent later in life. This
is the name under which most information was located.

# ACKNOWLEDGMENTS

We would like to thank the Tempe, Arizona, Public Library and the Arizona State University Library for their invaluable patience and assistance. We would also like to thank Leslie Swift and Alex Rossino in the photo archives at the United States Holocaust Memorial Museum. Many names and resources were gratefully received from historians and enthusiasts of the World War II era, including Anna and Chris Anderson, Scott Miller, Jeanine Sobieski, Diana Sluhan, and Sheila Jerusalem. We would also like to thank Brian Love for his editing skills and patience during the final revisions of the book.

# ABBREVIATIONS

Works frequently cited in the text have been identified by the following abbreviations:

| | |
|---|---|
| AmAu&B | *American Authors and Books* |
| AmM&WS | *American Men and Women of Science* |
| AmWomWr | *American Women Writers* |
| AnnObit | *Annual Obituary* |
| Au&Wr | *The Author's and Writer's Who's Who* |
| AuBYP Supp | *Authors of Books for Young People, Supplement* |
| Baker | *Baker's Biographical Dictionary of Musicians* |
| BioIn | *Biographical Index* |
| CelR | *Celebrity Register* |
| ConAu | *Contemporary Authors* |
| CurBio | *Current Biography* |
| CurBioYrbk | *Current Biography Yearbook* |
| DcAmB | *Dictionary of American Biography* |
| DcLB | *Dictionary of Literary Biography* |
| EncAB | *Encyclopedia of American Biography* |
| EncE | *Encyclopedia of Espionage* |
| EncHol | *Encyclopedia of the Holocaust* |
| EncTR | *Encyclopedia of the Third Reich* |
| EncWL | *Encyclopedia of World Literature in the Twentieth Century* |

| | |
|---|---|
| EncWT | *Encyclopedia of World War Two* |
| FilmgC | *The Filmgoers Companion* |
| ForWC | *Foremost Women in Communications* |
| GoodHS | *The Good Housekeeping Woman's Almanac* |
| HerW | *Her Way* |
| IntAu&W | *International Author's and Writer's Who's Who* |
| IntDcWB | *International Dictionary of Women's Biography* |
| IntWW | *The International Who's Who* |
| InWom | *Index to Women of the World* |
| InWomSup | *Index to Women of the World, Supplement* |
| LinLibL | *The Lincoln Library of Language Arts* |
| ModGL | *Modern German Literature* |
| MusS | *Musicians Since 1900* |
| NewEOP | *New Encyclopedia of the Opera* |
| NewYT | *New York Times* |
| NewYTBE | *New York Times Biographical Edition* |
| NewYTBS | *New York Times Biographical Service* |
| NotAW: Mod | *Notable American Women: The Modern Period* |
| OxAm | *The Oxford Companion to American Literature* |
| OxFilm | *The Oxford Companion to Film* |
| OxGer | *The Oxford Companion to German Literature* |
| REn | *The Reader's Encyclopedia* |
| REnAL | *The Reader's Encyclopedia of American Literature* |
| SmATA | *Something About the Author* |
| TwCA | *Twentieth Century Authors* |
| TwCA Supp | *Twentieth Century Authors, Supplement* |
| TwCW | *Twentieth Century Writing* |
| WebAB | *Webster's American Biographies* |
| WhAm | *Who Was Who in America* |
| WhE&EA | *Who Was Who Among English and European Authors* |
| Who | *Who's Who* |
| WhoAm | *Who's Who in America* |
| WhoAmW | *Who's Who of American Women* |
| WhoF | *Who's Who in France* |

| WhoHol | *Who's Who in the Holocaust* |
| WhoM | *Who's Who in Music* |
| WhoThe | *Who's Who in the Theatre* |
| WhoWJ | *Who's Who in World Jewry* |
| WhoWNG | *Who's Who in Nazi Germany* |
| WhoWor | *Who's Who in the World* |
| WhoWWII | *Who's Who in World War II* |
| WomA | *Women Artists* |
| WomPA | *Women in Public Affairs* |
| WorAl | *World Almanac Book of Who's Who* |
| WorAlB | *World Almanac Biographical Dictionary* |
| WorAu | *World Authors* |
| WrDr | *The Writer's Directory* |

# A

## ABEGG, ELISABETH

(1882–?)
**Rescuer, Germany**

Elisabeth Abegg was a German Quaker born in 1882 and raised in Strasbourg (Alsace). She relocated to Berlin and became a history teacher at the Luisen girls' school. When the Nazis came to power in 1933 she was dismissed because of her anti-Nazi protests. By 1942, she was hiding Jews in her home despite the fact that her bedridden mother and sickly sister as well as several Nazi party members lived in the same house. Since Jewish children were not allowed to attend school, she continued to teach them in her home. She helped dozens of Jews to escape with the help of Quaker friends, pastors, and former students. After hiding the refugees in Berlin, she helped them escape to Alsace, East Prussia, and Switzerland. She provided them with false identity papers and provisions by selling her own jewelry and belongings.

**BIBLIOGRAPHY**

Levner, H. D. *When Compassion Was a Crime*. London: Wolff, 1966; EncHol.

Elisabeth Abegg. Yad Vashem Photo Archives, courtesy of
USHMM Photo Archives.

# ADAMOWICZ, IRENA

**(1910–1963)**
**Underground Leader, Poland**

Irena Adamowicz, born in Warsaw in 1910, was among the leaders of
the Polish youth movement, developed to help Polish youngsters during
World War II. After receiving a degree in social work from Warsaw

Irena Adamowicz. Courtesy of USHMM Photo Archives.

University, she carried out social and educational work in the Ha-Shomer ha-Tsa'ir movement, a youth group started by the Jewish community to counter fear and suffering and to transport young people to safety. She became involved in the Jewish underground movement in the ghettos of Warsaw, Bialystok, Vilna, Kovno, and Siauliai (a city in Lithuanian S.S.R.), carrying messages and giving encouragement to the residents there. She helped establish contact between the Jewish underground and members of the Home Army.

After the end of the war she continued to have contact with many survivors of the pioneer Zionist movements in Poland and was named "Righteous Among Nations" by Yad Vashem in Jerusalem.

**BIBLIOGRAPHY**

EncHol.

# ADELSBERGER, LUCIE

**(1895–1971)**
**Physician, Camp Prisoner, Germany**

Lucie Adelsberger, a physician at Auschwitz, was born in Nuremberg in 1895. She studied medicine at the University of Erlangen and in 1927 joined the Institute Robert Koch in Berlin where she specialized in immunology and allergies, managing to practice privately and to conduct research at the Institute. She demonstrated the occurrence of antigen-antibody reactions in individuals with certain types of cancer, published many articles in medical journals, and received an international reputation. Harvard offered her a prominent faculty position in bacteriology in 1933, but she was unable to accept the invitation because she could not obtain a visa for her mother. When the Nazis came to power in 1933, Adelsberger lost the title of doctor and became a *Judenbehandler*, an attendant of Jews. She was one of the last Jews to be deported, leaving on a transport on May 17, 1943.

The Nazis took Adelsberger to Auschwitz, where she tended the sick in the Gypsy camp with neither medical equipment nor medicine. Adelsberger contracted typhus within a month of her arrival at Auschwitz. After her recovery, she returned to the Gypsy camp and continued working there until the liquidation of the Gypsies at the end of July 1944. The Nazis then assigned her to a group of children in the women's camp at Birkenau, again without any medicine or medical equipment. Some of her patients were twins used by Josef Mengele, the camp physician, for his infamous experiments.

In January 1945, as the Russians approached Auschwitz, approximately 60,000 inmates were set out on the infamous "death march." Adelsberger survived the march to Ravensbruck where the Allies eventually liberated her. She chronicled her experiences in a book entitled *Auschwitz: A Doctor's Life*, which was translated into English in 1995. She called the royalties blood money and sent the proceeds from the book to Israel for children whose parents had died at Auschwitz.

In 1949, she immigrated to the United States and worked at Montefiore

Hospital and Medical Center in New York for twenty-two years. Her view that the presence of changes in red blood cells indicated incipient cancer resulted in a large body of research for early detection of cancer. When grants from the Cancer Institute of the National Institutes of Health were not enough to pay for her research, she opened a private practice and used the income to continue her research. She died in 1971.

### BIBLIOGRAPHY

Adelsberger, Lucie. *Auschwitz: A Doctor's Life*. Boston: Northeastern University Press, 1995; *Bio-Base*; AmM&WS 76P; NewYTBE 71; WhoAmJ 66; WhoAmJ 68; AnnObit of 79; ConAu 33R; BioIn 9; obituary in NewYT, November 4, 1971, 48.

## ANDERSON, JANE

(1893–?)
**Nazi Propagandist, United States**

Known as "The Georgia Peach" when she broadcast Nazi propaganda during the 1940s, Jane Anderson was born Foster Anderson on January 6, 1893. Her father, Robert M. Anderson, was a frontier lawman and associate of Buffalo Bill Cody; her mother was Ellen Luckie Anderson. She lived in Atlanta, Georgia, until her mother's death when Jane was ten, then she lived with her grandmother in Demorest, Georgia. Anderson attended Piedmont College with fellow student Mei-ling Soong (Madame Chiang Kai-shek), then joined her father in Yuma, Arizona. She also attended Kidd-Key College in Sherman, Texas, but never graduated. She moved to New York hoping to sell her novels about the West. Anderson married Deems Taylor, a famous musicologist, but left him in the spring of 1915 and went to live in London. She became a war correspondent for the *Daily Mail* (London) and was the first woman to make a flight across London in one of His Majesty's "air machines." Soon she was flying over the English Channel and completing loop-the-loops over Hyde Park. She became friends with H. G. Wells, Joseph Conrad, diplomats in the British Foreign Office and the Quai d'Orsay in Paris, and with Japanese and Italian ambassadors.

Anderson continued her journalistic career after the First World War writing for magazines such as *Harper's, Collier's,* and *Century*. In 1933 she married a Spanish nobleman, the Marquis Alvarez de Cienfuegos, in a royal wedding in an ancient cathedral in Seville. On July 18, 1936, Francisco Franco's Nationalists invaded the Iberian Peninsula and headed toward Madrid. Anderson became a war correspondent again on the battlefront. The Nationalists captured her in September and tried her in Madrid on charges of espionage. She was found guilty and sentenced to death. She spent six weeks in political prisons where she was interrogated under blinding lights around the clock. Then she was suddenly released, gaunt from scurvy and with rat bites on her body.

Anderson managed to turn her experiences into a literary coup and in 1937 was invited to Washington, D.C. to speak. She became a propagandist for Franco and in 1940–41 went to Berlin when the Nazis offered her a radio show as "The Georgia Peach" or "Lady Haw Haw." Usually her programs consisted of descriptions of life in the Third Reich, accolades for Hitler, and condemnations of the American press. Her program aired until March 6, 1942, when, after describing a meal of sweets and champagne in a fine German restaurant, the U.S. Office of War Information rebroadcast her program back into the Reich. The program angered German citizens who were living on sparse rations. The Nazi authorities dismissed her editors and took her off the air.

Anderson emerged again on June 19, 1944, when it was announced that she was to return to Germany to cover the invasion. Afterwards, she and her husband fled to Austria where they hid for two years in the company of a former Gestapo agent. They tried to cross into Switzerland on April 2, 1947, and were arrested. Austria declined to prosecute and she returned to Madrid and was not heard of again.

**BIBLIOGRAPHY**

Shirer, William L. "The American Radio Traitors." *Harper's*, October 1943, 402; Schofield, William G. *Treason Trail*. New York: Rand McNally & Company, 1964, 203–4; Anderson, Jane, and Gordon Bruce. *Flying, Submarining and Mine Sweeping*. London: Sir Joseph Canston & Sons, 1916; Jane Anderson Files, FBI, Department of Justice, Washington, D.C.; Rolo, Charles J. *Radio Goes to War*. New York: G. P. Putnam's Sons, 1942; Ettlinger, Harold. *The Axis on the Air*. New York: Bobbs-Merrill Company, 1943; Edwards, John Carver. "Atlanta's Prodigal Daughter: The Turbulent Life of Jane Anderson as Ex-patriate and Nazi Propagandist." *The Atlantic Historical Journal* 28 (summer 1984): 23–42; Edwards, John Carver. "Jane Anderson Alias The Georgia Peach." In *Berlin Calling: American Broadcasters in Service to the Third Reich*. New York: Praeger, 1991; WhoAmJ 58; WhoAmJ 64.

# ARENDT, HANNAH

**(1906–1975)**
**Zionist, Resistance Worker, Germany**

Hannah Arendt was born to German Jews Paul Arendt, an engineer, and his wife Martha Cohn Arendt in Hanover, Germany, on October 14, 1906.

Hannah Arendt. Courtesy of USHMM Photo Archives.

She was reared and educated in Koenigsberg and attended the University of Heidelberg, majoring in philosophy. At age twenty-two, she received a Ph.D. degree from Heidelberg for her dissertation on St. Augustine. In September 1929, she married Gunther Stern, with whom she had been living, and continued her unconventional life, smoking cigars and spouting philosophy.

Her husband fled to Paris the day after the Reichstag was set on fire, February 27, 1933, but Arendt remained behind to become an active resister. She became involved with the Zionists and her apartment became a way station for fleeing enemies of Hitler on their way to various border crossings. In 1933 Kurt Blumenfeld of the German Zionist Organization asked her to do some illegal work at the Prussian State Library. Her task was to collect information that would show the extent of anti-Semitic actions in non-governmental organizations, private circles, business associations, and professional societies. The information was to be used at the Eighteenth Zionist Congress that summer in Prague.

Arendt had been working on the project for a few weeks and was on the way to lunch with her mother when the Nazis arrested them and took them to police headquarters at Alexanderplatz. They released the two women eight days later, but the Arendts now knew they would have to leave Germany as soon as possible. Since neither had travel documents, they fled by way of the thick forests in the Erzgebirge Mountains, known to Jews as "the Green Front." They made their way to Prague and crossed the Czechoslovakian border at night. They became "stateless persons" in Paris, where Arendt worked for social agencies from 1935 to 1939 for a French branch of the Youth Aliyah, a relief organization for placement of orphaned Jewish children in Palestine.

Arendt emigrated to the United States in 1940 when the Nazis invaded Paris. She became research director of the Conference on Jewish Relations from 1944 to 1946 and chief editor of Schocken Books from 1946 to 1948. From 1949 to 1952, she was executive secretary for the Jewish Cultural Reconstruction, Inc. organization, collecting and reallocating Jewish writings that the Nazis had seized and dispersed.

During this time she wrote *The Origin of Totalitarianism* (1951) and received a Guggenheim Fellowship in 1952. She pursued a scholarly life lecturing and teaching at prestigious universities such as Princeton, the University of California at Berkeley, the University of Chicago, and Brooklyn College. A second book, *The Human Condition*, was published in 1958. The next year she became the first woman full professor at Princeton as a visiting professor. The lectures she gave there were published as a collection called *On Revolution* in 1963. In the spring of 1961, Arendt attended the trial of Adolf Eichmann in Jerusalem as a reporter for *The New Yorker*. She prepared the information from the trial into a book entitled *Eichmann in Jerusalem: A Report on the Banality of Evil*, published in 1964. The book was very controversial because she argued that Adolf Eichmann was normal given the society in which he lived, and she alienated many friends as a result.

Arendt was a professor at the University of Chicago's Committee on Social Thought from 1963 to 1967 and wrote essays and lectured during this time. Some of these essays were collected in *Crisis of the Republic* published in 1972. Hannah Arendt died of a heart attack on December 4, 1975. Her last book, *The Life of the Mind*, was published posthumously in 1979.

## BIBLIOGRAPHY

"Biographical Note." *Saturday Review of Literature* 334, March 24, 1951, 10; obituary in *Publisher's Weekly*, December 15, 1975, 26; obituary in *Time*, December 15, 1975, 64; True, M. "Hannah Arendt and the Renewal of Our Common World." *America*, January 13, 1976, 23–24; Young-Bruehl, Elisabeth. *Hannah Arendt: For Love of the World*. New Haven: Yale University Press, 1984; Botstein, L. "Hannah Arendt: The Jewish Question." *New Republic* 179, October 21, 1978, 32+; Papers, manuscripts, correspondence of more than 30,000 items in the Library of Congress; CurBio 59; IntWW 76N; AnnObit of 79; InWom; IntAu&W 76, 77; IntWW 74; WhoAmJ 61, 64, 66, 68, 70, 72, 74; WhoWor 72, 76; AmAu&B; AmWomWr; BioIn 2, 5, 8, 10, 11, 12; ConAu 61; NotAW: Mod.

# ASTRUP, HELEN

(1900–?)
**Resistance Fighter, Norway**

In February 1941, Helen Astrup was a widow of British nationality living in a German-controlled country. Her husband, Carsten Astrup, was a Norwegian sea captain on an oil tanker; his ship had been torpedoed off the coast of Ireland. When the Nazis invaded Oslo in April 1940, Helen lost her London income and she and her eight-year-old daughter, Kirsti, were living on bread and turnips.

Nils Berg, a member of the Joessings Resistance fighters, contacted Astrup. She began by distributing Resistance newsletters despite the fact that anyone caught by quislings or Nazis while in possession of such materials would automatically be sent to prison camps. Eventually, Resistance officials gave her the responsibility of claiming the "body" of her Jewish neighbor, Frau Hirschfeldt, from the hospital morgue. In reality, they were smuggling Hirschfeldt and her daughter out of Norway and into Sweden enclosed in the coffin. Germans stopped them and the trucks were confiscated. The coffin was placed on the side of the road until such time as the trucks returned. She sat casually on the coffin chatting with the Germans until the trucks returned, and eventually got the two women to Sweden.

Astrup was next ordered to use her apartment so Resistance fighters could make a raid on a wealthy quisling who lived nearby. She was to wave a red cloth if anything went wrong, however, since authorities arrived so quickly, she could only watch helplessly as they killed three of her co-workers. Eventually she and the others escaped.

Astrup volunteered her summer home at Larkollen on the Fjord to help hide gold until the Resistance could smuggle it out of the country. Unknown enemies pursued her and the man smuggling the gold out, but they managed to evade them and make it to the summer cabin. She was left alone in the cabin and hid in the oven as the pursuers searched for the gold. She escaped after a shootout with the pursuers and made her way back to Oslo.

After Astrup returned to Oslo, the Resistance gave her the task of determining whether an Englishman named Frobisher could be trusted. She arranged a meeting, then watched as another agent approached him. Suddenly Nazis appeared from all directions; Frobisher was a traitor but Astrup managed to escape undetected. When she returned home, friends told her that she and her daughter would be leaving immediately. They were taken to a farmhouse along with several other women and children. They walked to the border and spent a week within "rifle shot" of Sweden. Their guides had refused to show them the way out because the Germans were bringing troops into the area. Astrup decided to go on by herself along with her daughter and a woman named Irma Jensen who had fled arrest for carrying newsletters. They hid their packs in the bushes and continued along the road. Germans stopped them but thought they were local and let them make their way across the pasture into Sweden. Astrup eventually settled in London; Jensen became a translator in Washington, D.C.

**BIBLIOGRAPHY**

Astrup, Helen, and B. L. Jacot. *Oslo Intrigue: A Woman's Memoir of the Norwegian Resistance*. New York: McGraw-Hill Book Company, 1954; Astrup, Helen. "Intrigue in Oslo." In *Women in the Resistance and in the Holocaust: The Voices of Eyewitnesses*, edited by Vera Laska, Westport, Conn.: Greenwood Press, 1983, 121–27.

# B

## BANCROFT, MARY

(1903–?)
**Swiss Spy, United States**

Mary Bancroft was born on October 29, 1903, to Hugh and Mary Cogan Bancroft. She was brought up by grandparents in Cambridge, Massachusetts, and lived an upper-class existence of trips to Europe, coming-out parties, and college at Smith. She left Smith to marry Sherwin C. Badger in 1923, but they divorced in 1932. She was living in Switzerland with her second husband, Jean Rufenacht, and working and studying with psychologist Carl Jung when World War II broke out. In 1942, she was recruited in Switzerland by Allen Dulles, head of the Office of Strategic Services and later head of the Central Intelligence Agency. Her first task was to contact Anna Siemsen, who in 1933 had been a professor of pedagogy at the University of Jena before being dismissed for signing a protest against the firing of another professor. Siemsen was later able to flee to Switzerland.

In 1943 Bancroft began translating a book by Hans Gisevius, a member of the Canaris organization, the intelligence service of the German Army known as the Abwehr. While working with Gisevius, she was supposed to find out if he was a double agent. Bancroft was able to obtain first-hand information on the burning of the Reichstag; the removal of General von Fritsch, commander-in-chief of the German Army, on charges of homosexuality; and the dismissal of Field Marshal von Blomberg as minister of war because his new wife was a convicted prostitute. She became aware of the many attempts by generals and high-placed civilians to remove Hitler from office. Gisevius was among those involved in the July 20, 1944, attempt on Hitler's life, after which Dulles smuggled him out of Germany.

In the spring of 1945 Bancroft was at the Nuremberg trials when Gisevius appeared as a witness. She immigrated to the United States in 1953 to become a journalist and freelance writer. She was also involved in New York Democratic politics.

### BIBLIOGRAPHY

Bancroft, Mary. *Autobiography of a Spy.* New York: William Morrow, 1983; WhoAmJ 61.

# BAR ONI, BRYNA

(1925–   )
**Partisan Fighter, Poland**

Bryna Bar Oni was born in Byten, Poland, in 1925. Her father was a mill builder and her mother operated a dry goods store. In 1938 she left home to attend a commercial high school in Baranowicze, but returned to Byten the next year as conditions in Poland worsened. The Russians entered Byten where the Bar Oni family was living and they then had to share their house with two Russian secretaries. Bryna was interrogated for black marketing after she sold a piece of leather to one of the secretaries. In June 1941 Bryna was forced to work at the railway station loading and unloading logs and freight, chopping wood, washing floors, and carrying water. She was forced to live in one room in the Byten ghetto.

In May 1942 Bar Oni learned of a partisan movement being organized in nearby Wolczenory woods. When the Germans destroyed the ghetto, she escaped by hiding in the attic under rags. She and her sister Yentl and Yentl's baby fled to the woods and joined the partisans. They made a camp and started a communal kitchen and kindergarten. Meanwhile the Nazis had liquidated all the Jews in Byten and the partisans were becoming more aggressive, organizing themselves into three groups— sabotaging the enemy, providing food, and guarding the woods. Bar Oni was the only female in the camp assigned to eight-hour shifts of guard duty. On September 18, the partisans were attacked and she and about 100 others fled deeper into the woods, sometimes covering ten miles in one day. While fleeing, she accidentally smothered a baby as she ran, and her sister and niece were killed in an ambush.

As the partisan ranks increased, anti-Semites infiltrated the ranks and the chief of staff ordered all Jews to leave the woods or be shot. Bar Oni was once more forced to flee. She lay camouflaged during the day and lived on stolen potatoes at night. Her feet were covered in rags and her body was covered in boils, but when she asked a farmer to give her salt for the boils, she was captured by the Germans. She refused to divulge any information and was released. She eventually found her original group and even though it was rumored she was dying of tuberculosis, they let her collect guns and supply food for the chief of staff. When a high-ranking partisan offered her group six guns if she would join his camp, she refused.

In the summer of 1943 an epidemic of typhus ran rampant throughout the partisan camps. Bar Oni contracted the disease in March 1944. For fourteen days she was near death, and by the time she returned to health she was completely bald, emaciated, and was even said to have lost her freckles. In July 1944 the Russians invaded the area and of the 370 Jews who had escaped the Byten ghetto, she was one of twenty-three remaining. Bar Oni wandered throughout the countryside in her brother-in-law's shoes trying to find a Jewish community. In the spring of 1946 she learned of a displaced person's camp near Nuremberg. The Germans arrested her on her way there and while being questioned about the whereabouts of her friends, she began throwing up blood. She was tried as a partisan, but the case was dismissed. She spent another two years in Germany until, on April 11, 1947, she was allowed to join relatives in America. She eventually married and settled in Chicago.

**BIBLIOGRAPHY**

Bar Oni, Bryna. "Life Among the Partisans." In *Women in the Resistance and in the Holocaust: The Voices of Eyewitnesses*, edited by Vera Laska, 271–78. Westport, Conn.: Greenwood Press, 1983; Bar Oni, Bryna. *The Vapor*. Chicago, Ill.: Visual Impact, 1976.

# BERGNER, ELISABETH

**(1897 or 1900–1986)**
**Actress, Germany**

Despite being Jewish, Elisabeth Bergner was one of the most important film stars during the Third Reich. She was born in 1897 or 1900 in Vi-

Elisabeth Bergner. New York World-Telegram & Sun collection.

enna, Austria. She studied at the Conservatoire from 1915 to 1919. She made her stage debut in Zurich in 1916 as Rosalind in *As You Like It*, followed by roles in other classics, including *Hamlet* in which she appeared as Ophelia. In 1923 she appeared as St. Joan in her first film, *Der Evangeliman*. Other roles made her one of the most prolific actresses on the continent, and in 1928 she toured Holland, Denmark, Sweden, Germany, and Austria. In 1931 she married director Paul Czinner and the two left Austria.

In 1933 Bergner made her stage debut in London in *Escape Me Never*. Then in 1934 Bergner returned to Berlin for the opening of *Catharine the Great*, a British film. The Nazi censor passed the film and the premiere attracted a fashionable crowd of Germans and foreign diplomats. However, when the first celebrities arrived, rioters began yelling, "Down with the Jew," and spattered eggs on posters in the lobby. They tried to prevent the theatergoers from entering the theater. The police had to escort them inside. Col. Ernest Roehm, leader of the Storm Troopers, speaking for Hitler, took the stage and begged the audience to remember that Germany was a land of law and order. The film went on to rave reviews but the next day it was withdrawn and the Minister of Propaganda, Joseph Goebbels, informed Bergner that she could no longer make films in Germany. She found that the event occurred three days after Goebbels had announced that non-Aryans, previously banned from German theaters, had been reappearing; he "requested" German authorities to prevent such lawbreaking and if the request was ignored, declared that the public might resort to "self-help to defend itself."

In 1935 Bergner went to New York and signed a contract with United Artists and began making American movies. In 1940 she contracted to make *The 49th Parallel* with Lawrence Olivier and Leslie Howard in Britain. The location shots were completed in Canada, but she did not return to Britain for the interiors and the film had to begin over with Glynis Johns. Critics chastised her for her ingratitude to Britain and hinted that she had feared arrest if Hitler invaded Britain. As late as 1950 she was not welcome in that country, and her career never regained its momentum. Elisabeth Bergner died on May 12, 1986, in London of undisclosed causes.

## BIBLIOGRAPHY

Shipman, David. *The Great Movie Stars: The Golden Years*. New York: Crown Publishers, 1970; "Mob Stops Film Starring Jewess." *Newsweek*, May 17, 1934, 15; EncTR; BioIn 5, 7, 9; EncWT; FilmgC; InWom; Who 82, 83; AnnObit of 86.

# BOHEC, JEANNE

(?–?)
**Resistance Fighter, France**

Jeanne Bohec, who taught the making of explosives to agents and led sabotage operations in her home province of Brittany, was a chemistry student working at a gunpowder factory when World War II began. On June 18, 1940 she obtained passage on a small tugboat and immigrated to England. She worked as a nanny until on January 6, 1941, Gen. Charles de Gaulle started a women's corps; Jeanne was among the first French volunteers to join. She received her basic training at the British Auxiliary Territorial Services school and was given the job of nurse's aid. She felt she was wasting her talent for dealing with chemicals and explosives and by persevering was finally allowed to become the only woman chemist in a laboratory that made explosives using common chemicals bought at the local pharmacy.

Eventually, Bohec was asked to return to France and work with the BCRA (Bureau Central de Renseignements et d'Action). Officials complained that the BCRA was no place for a woman and again she persevered until she became the first female agent. She attended the all-male sabotage school in Scotland and received weapons training in pistols, revolvers, daggers, and submachine guns, and explosives training in jelly-plastic detonators and delayed-action devices. After attending parachute school in Ringway, England, the BCRA outfitted her with all French belongings, and in January 1944, they gave her the code name "Rateau" (Rake).

Bohec boarded a Lysander for a first attempt to land in France, but the landing was aborted because there were no lights on the field; the second was canceled because of bad weather. Finally she was parachuted from a bomber wearing civilian clothes including her handbag, which hung around her neck. She landed in Brittany and began instructing agents in the use of explosives and arranging drops of armaments from Britain. Under the code name "Green Plan," she was in charge of cutting railway lines from Dinan to Questembert. On May 6, she was a member of a team of five who placed explosive charges in railroad switchings.

After D-Day, Bohec joined the French Forces of the Interior and lived in a forest camp outside the town of Saint Marcel. In June 1944, a German patrol discovered the camp and attacked at dawn. She coded an urgent telegram to London and asked for additional submachine guns; she was refused. She set off on her bicycle to deliver a message to another unit but was stopped by German soldiers on horses. She convinced them she was a harmless civilian and continued on. As a result, RAF planes bombed the remaining 3,000 tons of ammunition, 500 Germans, and thirty fighter planes. In retaliation, 600 civilians in a nearby town were massacred in the local church. She moved to Quimper for a general insurrection but officials refused to give her a weapon. She rode in a tank instead and fired a bazooka.

After liberation, Bohec returned to England and worked at BCRA headquarters. She returned to France in September 1944, when the BCRA moved their headquarters there. In May 1945, she received the Resistance Medal and later the Cross of the Chevalier of Legion of Honor as well as a commendation from General Eisenhower for brave conduct. She married, divorced, and became a single parent and teacher in Paris.

### BIBLIOGRAPHY

Saywell, Shelley. "Le Rescau: France, 1939–45." *Women in War* (32–73). New York: Viking Penguin, Inc., 1985.

## BRAUN, EVA

**(1912–1945)**
**Mistress of Hitler, Germany**

Eva Braun, the mistress of Adolf Hitler, was born in 1912 and educated by English nuns. After school she became a sales assistant to a photographer, Heinrich Hoffman. It was in Hoffman's shop that she first met Adolf Hitler in 1929. She became Hitler's mistress in 1932 and it was apparently not a happy relationship since she tried to commit suicide several times. In 1936 she moved from Hitler's apartment in Munich to his house at Berchtesgaden, where she served as his hostess. When the Russians invaded Berlin in April 1945, she joined Hitler in his specially constructed underground bunker in Berlin. On April 29, 1945, they were married and the next day she committed suicide by taking poison; Hitler then shot himself. The common theory is that she was buried with him in the Chancellery Garden above the bunker.

### BIBLIOGRAPHY

Boore, Herbert, and James Wyman, eds. *Who Killed Hitler?* New York: Booktab Press, 1947; Braun, Eva. *Private Life of Adolph Hitler: Intimate Notes and Diary,* edited by Paul Tabori. New York: Aldor, 1949; Infeld, Glenn B. *Eva and Adolf.* New York: Grosset and Dunlap, 1974; AnnObit of 79; BioIn 2, 4, 5, 8, 9, 10; EncTR; IntDcWB; WhoWWII; WorAu.

## BRAUNSTEINER, HERMINE

(1920–  )
**Nazi Camp Guard, Germany**

Hermine Braunsteiner, a female guard in Nazi death camps, was made supervisor of Ravensbruck concentration camp in Germany in 1941. In 1943 she became the supervising warden in the extermination camp of Majdanek near Lublin, in German-occupied Poland. In 1949 an Austrian court convicted her of murder, including assassination, manslaughter, and infanticide, and she was sentenced to three years in prison. After her release, an Austrian civil court granted her amnesty from further prosecution in Austria.

In 1959 Braunsteiner married Russell Ryan, an American electrical construction engineer, and moved to New York City. In 1963 she became an American citizen. However, a deportation hearing was begun and evidence was presented by survivors of concentration camps that she had terrorized, tortured, and murdered inmates. They testified that she was involved in the selection process for the gas chambers and even identified some who had been overlooked. Witnesses said she assaulted a female inmate who died the next day and ordered a young girl to stand on a stool so SS guards could hang her. She retaliated that she had only performed her job.

In 1971 the courts stripped her of American citizenship on the premise that she had failed to report service in German concentration camps on her application for American residence and citizenship. On March 14, 1973, an extradition bench warrant was issued in Dusseldorf that ordered her to stand trial in a German court without bail. U.S. marshals arrested her at her home and she became the first U.S. resident to be extradited for alleged war crimes. It is unknown what happened to her after her extradition.

**BIBLIOGRAPHY**

EncTR.

# BREWDA, ALINA

(1905– )
Physician, Camp Prisoner, Poland

Born in Warsaw, Poland, of Jewish heritage in 1905, Alina Brewda completed her medical studies at the University of Warsaw in 1930. She became an unpaid doctor at Wolsky General Hospital in the poorest
section of Warsaw and at L'Hôpital Bretenneau in Paris until she was
granted the position of junior houseman (doctor attached to a hospital),
which carried a small salary. She spent ten months with Professor Jean-
Louis Fauré, one of the most famous gynecologists in the world. In 1932
she returned to Warsaw to a small obstetrical hospital with twenty-five
beds and worked as a part-time assistant at another hospital as well.
She fought for contraception, built up a private practice, and edited a
monthly journal for doctors, nurses, and midwives called *Voice of the
Midwives*. When the Nazis came to power, they no longer allowed her
to treat non-Jews and moved her into the Warsaw ghetto where she
again became an unpaid medical worker. It was a testimony to her pop-
ularity that her former Aryan patients visited her in the ghetto; hus-
bands often led her into underground tunnels to treat their pregnant
wives.

In July 1942 Brewda was arrested by German soldiers just as she was
beginning an operation. As she was pushed forward in the crowd of
other prisoners through the streets, her brother's friends suddenly
grabbed her and pulled her into a nearby building. They gave her a
nurse's uniform and she remained free, but in September she was arrested again. She managed to escape and her brother arranged for an
ambulance to smuggle her out of the city. The Germans caught her and
ordered her to stand against a wall with seven other people. Six had
been shot when they came to her. They were out of ammunition and
took Brewda and the remaining prisoner to an old school next to a hospital. Brewda, wearing her white doctor's coat, managed to sneak out to
the hospital next door at four in the morning. She stayed there for four
days until the hospital was evacuated and she managed to get back to
the ghetto. She was arrested again along with her brother and sister-in-
law. Her sister-in-law managed to escape, but her brother died at Treblinka.

Brewda was sent to Majdanek concentration camp where authorities took her to the Aryan section and gave her full status as a doctor. She began smuggling women from the Jewish section over to the Aryan section where she performed abortions and thus saved their lives. She cared for 300 Greek women who had contracted typhoid and typhus. Sometimes four to ten died in one day, but she did not record their deaths for twenty-four hours so that she could continue to receive their rations to feed the surviving patients. Meanwhile, officials sent word to Berlin praising her work; unfortunately, it resulted in bringing her to the attention of authorities and they transferred her to Auschwitz on September 21, 1943. Majdanek was abandoned a few weeks later and most of the women were sent to the gas chambers.

Brewda was taken to Auschwitz, then Birkenau where she received tattoo no. 62761. She was sent to Block 10 where Dr. Carl Clauberg was conducting experiments on the sterilization of Jews with overdoses of X rays. Brewda contracted pneumonia and was treated by Dr. Dorota Kleinova, who had been sent to Auschwitz for activities in the French Resistance, and a young SS doctor named Munch. Brewda would later provide a deposition for Munch at his criminal war trial that helped acquit him. Along with Dr. Kleinova and Dr. Adelaide Hautval, Brewda would also be a witness in the libel trial of Leon Uris, author of *Exodus*, initiated by Dr. Wladyslaw Dering who claimed that all he could do was comfort the women as their ovaries were removed without anesthetics, since he would have been shot if he had refused to help. Prosecutors pointed out that all three female doctors had refused to cooperate and had worked to lessen the women's suffering.

In January 1944, Brewda suffered a heart attack and was told to stay in bed for weeks; three days later she was treating her patients again and lying about the extent of their illnesses to keep them from the gas chambers. She eventually joined the Communist underground movement known as the Auschwitz Fighting Group, although she did not become a Communist. She gained access to the SS dispensary and stole drugs. During a typhus epidemic, contact between the various groups in other areas was cut off. Brewda solved the problem by suggesting that young female prisoners be trained as nurses. Thirty-six women, mostly wives and sisters of underground workers, became nurses and contact was resumed.

Brewda continued her work until January 18, 1945, when the evacuation of Auschwitz began. Brewda and Kleinova hid with a group of women prisoners too ill to walk and risked being blown up after the evacuation. The Nazis discovered them, however, and made them join the march of 60,000 prisoners through harsh winter weather. When guards prodded her with bayonets and told her to run or be shot, other prisoners took her arms on both sides and carried her. She and Kleinova were put in a cattle car and taken to Ravensbruck, then Neustadt-Glewe. When the Allies liberated the camp on May 8, 1945, Brewda was in the operating room. After liberation, she set up a hospital for 200 patients in a nearby village. Kleinova managed to get to Cracow, where she wandered aimlessly through the streets until a former patient took her to an apartment where she had her first bath in years.

In September 1945, Brewda suffered a coronary thrombosis at age forty. For nine months she was bedridden. Meanwhile, she managed to contact an uncle in London, and on February 22, 1947, she arrived in England where she resumed practicing medicine.

### BIBLIOGRAPHY

Minney, Rubeigh J. *I Shall Fear No Evil: The Story of Dr. Alina Brewda*. London: Kimber, 1966.

## BROUSSE, AMY ELIZABETH

(1910–1963)
**British Spy, United States**

Called the "war's greatest unsung heroine" by Sir William Stephenson, Canadian millionaire-industrialist and director of British Intelligence activities and special operations in the Western Hemisphere, Brousse operated under the code name of "Cynthia" and worked for British Security Co-ordination. Born in Minneapolis, Minnesota, on November 22, 1910, Brousse was presented at Buckingham Palace and made her social debut in Washington, D.C. Her father was Major George Cyrus Thorpe, U.S. Marine Corps, and her mother was Cora Wells Thorpe, educated at Columbia University, the Sorbonne, and the University of Munich. Brousse married Arthur Pack, commercial counselor of the British Legation in Santiago, Chile, and second secretary on the commercial side of the British Embassy in Washington.

In 1937 Pack was transferred to Warsaw and suffered a cerebral thrombosis. He was sent to a London nursing home to recover, and during this time Brousse began passing information to British Intelligence gathered from the Polish social circles to which she belonged. On a visit to Prague she obtained a map showing Hitler's plans for further aggression. In April 1939 her husband was fully recovered and they were sent to Chile. Carlos Prendis, the editor of *La Nacion*, approached her about writing propaganda articles for the Allies. Her first article, "The Polish Corridor," appeared on September 1, 1939. On September 21, 1939 she also began writing for the *South Pacific Mail*, an English-language newspaper. She wrote for ten months but began receiving threatening letters and the German ambassador demanded she be expelled, so she quit.

In 1940 she left Pack in Chile and returned to New York, where she joined British Security Co-ordination and received the code name of "Cynthia." They told her to go to Washington, D.C., and act as a hostess at parties as a way of obtaining information. She was asked especially to contact a former suitor, Alberto Lais, an admiral and Italian naval attaché. In March 1941 Lais confessed that he had given orders for all Italian merchant ships in American ports to be sabotaged to prevent embargoing by the United States. She reported the information but of the twenty-seven Italian ships in ports twenty-five had already been badly damaged and needed extensive repairs. Lais was expelled, but he gave Brousse the name and address of his assistant in charge of the cipher room in the Naval attaché's office and she was able to procure vital ciphers for the British.

Brousse's next assignment was in March 1942. Her superiors ordered her to obtain Vichy French naval ciphers as a preliminary to the British–American invasion of North Africa. She approached an assistant to the chief cipher officer and he turned her in. She managed to talk her way out of it, and then went in with a safecracker. They ran out of time. They went back a second night, but the safe would not open. She spent the next day practicing with the safecracker, went in a third time, and photographed the ciphers herself.

Brousse was sent to France in the summer of 1944, but by this time her cover was blown and she was forced to retire. She married Charles Brousse, a press attaché for the Embassy of the Republic of France whom she had met during her espionage days. They settled in a medieval castle in the Pyrénées, where she lived until December 1, 1963, when she died of cancer.

## BIBLIOGRAPHY

Hyde, H. Montgomery. *Cynthia*. New York: Farrar, Straus and Giroux, 1965; "Blond Bond." *Time*, December 20, 1963, 17.

# BUTLER, JOSEPHINE

(?–?)
**British Spy, Great Britain**

Josephine Butler was born in Buckinghamshire, England. She had six brothers, four of whom died in active service during World War II. She received her education from governesses and graduated as a doctor of medicine from the Sorbonne in Paris. She joined the Cancer Research Unit, a private clinic in Paris, but in 1938 returned to Britain. Butler joined FANY (First Aid Nursing Yeomanry), then MEW (Ministry of Economic Warfare), where she worked with maps.

Eventually Butler began translating secret reports from France for the Theatre Intelligence Service, and in February 1942 Winston Churchill asked her to become the only woman member of his secret circle, a group of twelve who were obtaining information to help set up the second front for the liberation of Europe. As a member of the secret circle, agents taught her how to drop out of a moving monoplane (knocking two front teeth out in the process); soft-karate, a killing method of the Samurai; and how to transmit and receive radio messages. In July 1942 a mono-plane glided over a field in France and Butler dropped out. She made her way to Paris, used her photographic memory to pick up information, then returned to England.

In November she returned to France to form an escape route for VIPs from Paris, and in December she returned to Paris to form resistance groups. During these and subsequent trips, she survived many danger-ous experiences. The Gestapo arrested her for crushing out a cigarette thrown by a Gestapo officer and sentenced her to two days in prison. Another time she had to cross the Cher River with two underground workers on each side of her because she could not swim. In February 1943 Butler was sent to bring out a Frenchman working for the Germans. When they got to Limoges, the man was shot and she and three other freedom fighters were hidden in a wine cellar by a Frenchman. He nailed the door shut behind them and when the Germans searched the house, they did not look in the cellar because the man had used old, rusted nails and the Germans concluded the door had been sealed for a long time.

Butler's next assignment, in October 1943, was to investigate the type of cement that the Germans were using for the Atlantic wall. She found the man who was an expert on the cement. His firm believed he was dead, but in actuality he was working for the Germans. She was in his hotel room when he realized she was an agent. Two of her men entered through the window, knocking him out, and on her way downstairs she ran into the Gestapo. They became suspicious and she went into the restroom. She bit off a cyanide capsule just in case, then using karate, burst through the window and escaped. Butler got her men back to the plane, but she had to stay behind because the plane was too light to carry all of them. She made her way back to the coast, hiding during the day and walking during the night. She had covered more than 300 miles and was dehydrated by the time she made it back to London.

Butler followed that 1944 assignment with one where she looked into reports that parts for a pilotless plane were being developed in Paris and that a mushroom cellar was being used to build a bomb that could fly— the V1, called the doodle bug by the British. In May 1944 she returned from London to Caen, France, to contact the headmistress of a residential school for forty children with tuberculosis where she could hide while finding out where Rommel was deploying his tanks. On May 28, however, the Panzers took over the school and trapped her during the invasion and bombing. (The glider pilot who had transported her throughout the war was shot down and killed on his return to England.) On June 2, the children were collected and taken to safety and she escaped. She spent the rest of the war hiding in the woods and helping refugees.

### BIBLIOGRAPHY

Butler, Josephine. *Churchill's Secret Agent*. Devon, England: Blaketon-Hall Ltd., 1983.

# C

## CAPPONI, CARLA

(1926– )
**Partisan Fighter, Italy**

Carla Capponi, called "the little English girl" because she was blonde, was an Italian partisan who operated in the underground. She worked as a translator and typist in Rome in a chemical laboratory to support her widowed mother and younger brothers and sisters as World War II began. She, along with Marisa Musu, formed the female section of the local Communist Party in Rome. She distributed subversive literature and organized public demonstrations and strikes against the existing government.

When World War II began, Capponi became a Gappista (member of GAP—Groups of Partisan Action) organized by Ilio Barontini, a former Tuscan railway worker. The group trained its members to use explosives and used the women to carry the bombs and set them off because they believed women were less suspicious looking. Among her activities as a Gappista, Capponi took part in the attack on Rome's main prison, Gegina Coeli, and an attack on the opera house containing 1,500 German soldiers. On March 7, 1944, she was identified as one of the Resistance members who blew up a German fuel truck carrying 2,500 gallons of gasoline, and she was placed on a wanted list put out by the Nazis. On March 23, 1944, she helped plan an attack on a specially trained anti-partisan unit in Rome. The partisans planned to attack the unit as they moved through a narrow street, Via Rasella. A bomb placed in a rubbish cart by partisan members killed thirty-three men and wounded seventy others. Hitler issued orders to kill ten Romans for every German killed in the ambush. Capponi and the other partisans went into hiding. On June 1, 1944, Capponi was told to return to Rome as the Americans approached the city to liberate it, and her Resistance days came to an end.

In 1948 relatives of the Roman civilians killed by the Germans at the Ardeatine affair filed a legal suit against the partisans, including Capponi. The court decided the action was a legitimate act of war and she was not held liable; however, the controversy over the affair was to plague her for most of her life. Even in the 1950s she was still receiving hate mail and obscene phone calls from relatives who blamed her for their loved ones' deaths. Still, she continued to be active in politics, becoming deputy of the Communist Party in 1953. In 1954 she lost a lung from an undisclosed disease and spent seven years in a sanitorium. No information is available from later in her life.

### BIBLIOGRAPHY

Saywell, Shelley. "Via Raselia: Italy, 1939–45." In *Women in War* (73–101). New York: Viking Penguin Inc., 1985.

## CARRÉ, MATHILDE-LILY

(1908–  )
**French Spy, France**

Mathilde-Lily Carré, one of the most notorious Allied spies of World War II, was born on June 29, 1908, in Creusot, France. She attended Lycée Victor Hugo in Paris in 1924 and obtained a teacher's certificate in 1932. She married a director of schools in Ain-Sefra in West Algeria and the two moved there. In 1939 her husband was sent to Syria and she returned to France to begin nursing studies to help the war effort. Carré was assigned to a military surgical hospital on the outskirts of Paris, and on May 10 she was asked to create an emergency dressing-station at Beauvais. She received a medal from the Minister of National Defense after the town was bombed.

In 1940 Roman Czerniawski recruited Carré to help him as he created a spy system in France's free zone. She was to transmit information that secret agents had obtained. He assigned her the pseudonym of "the Cat." She went to Paris when the Office of Military Intelligence (called Inter-allié) was organized and was given increasingly more difficult tasks including recruiting new agents.

On November 17, 1941, the Germans arrested Carré and placed her in Santé prison. They told her she would be shot unless she cooperated and insisted she continue to pick up her messages each day and meet with her fellow agents as the Germans listened in. Hugo Bleicher, the agent in charge of Carré, insisted she live with him, threatening to arrest her mother and father if she did not. Meanwhile she continued to send messages to London, where agents put her in charge of organizing a fictitious resistance network. London gave her 10,000 francs and allowed her to live in Paris.

Bleicher sent her to England to obtain the names of French agents for the Allies. Carré and another agent planned to bring back explosives and poison to kill Bleicher. The landing craft that picked her up capsized and after two other abortive tries she was finally picked up on February 26, 1942. When she was in London in July she was arrested and imprisoned for the rest of the war under orders from the French. She remained in prison until June 1, 1945, when she was returned to France and imprisoned. She remained in Fresnes prison until she went on trial on January 3, 1949. She was sentenced to death, but on May 4, the President of the Republic commuted the sentence to hard labor for life. On August 2, 1952, Carré's life sentence for hard labor was commuted to twenty years hard labor dating from July 1, 1942. She converted to Catholicism and obtained an early release on September 7, 1954. She wrote an account of her adventures in 1959 entitled *I Was "the Cat,"* which was published in the United States in 1967.

### BIBLIOGRAPHY

Carré, Mathilde-Lily. *I Was "the Cat."* London: Horwitz, 1967; EncE 75; BioIn 5, 8, 10, 11; WhoWWII.

## CHEVRILLON, CLAIRE

(1907–   )
**Resistance Fighter, France**

Claire Chevrillon was born in 1907 to André Chevrillon, called the "first literary critic" in France; her mother was Clarisse Porges Chevrillon.

When the war began, her mother and father sheltered anti-Nazi refugees in their large house in Saint-Cloud. They escorted women and children out of Paris until 1940 when the Germans requisitioned their home and the Luftwaffe used it as a barracks.

In October 1942, Chevrillon was an English teacher at the College Sevigné, a well-known girls' school in Paris, when she discovered the underground movement. She joined the Paris Air Operations and later the Code Service. She began by receiving mail, phone calls, packages, and messages for agents. In April 1943, Pont-Blanc police arrested her and took her to Paris where the Gestapo interrogated her. She was placed in Fresnes prison from April to June then returned to Pont-Blanc, no longer useful to the underground. She arrived in Bordeaux and made several illegal crossings of the demarcation line of the German Occupation troops. She changed her name to Christiane Clouet, resigned her teaching job, and returned to working with the underground in the coding section of the Delegation in France of the French Committee of National Liberation.

She was a code clerk from October 1943 to January 1944. During that time, she saw couriers twice a day to receive messages that needed encoding or decoding despite the fact that radio operators were the most often arrested of the Delegation's agents. From January to June 1944 she headed the Code Service, the main link in communications to Gen. Charles de Gaulle's Free French Government in London. She used small silk handkerchiefs to encode and decode messages; each had 120 rows of numbers, which were the keys to encoding or decoding the messages.

As D-Day approached, her work became even more dangerous as the messages became longer and more frequent. In addition, she traveled to many towns on her bicycle, teaching new coders and preparing safe houses for agents in transit. She worked for the United Nations Relief and Repatriation Association in Germany in 1945, helping refugees to find their way back to France, Belgium, and the Netherlands.

After the war, Chevrillon taught at the College Sevigné in 1946 and Bristol University in 1947 in England. She returned to Paris in 1948 and supervised Bristol's French students. In 1957, the French cultural attaché in Morocco invited her to set up a cultural center in Fez, and in 1969 she went to Tunis to set up the French Cultural Library. She retired in 1972 and returned to Paris.

## BIBLIOGRAPHY

Chevrillon, Claire. *Code Name Christiane Clouet: A Woman in the French Resistance.* College Station: Texas A & M University Press, 1995.

# COHN, MARIANNE

(1924–1944)
Resistance Fighter, Germany

On Wednesday, June 1, 1944, Marianne Cohn, member of the Eclaireurs Israelites de France (French Jewish Scouts), was preparing to cross into Switzerland near Lyon, France, with a convoy of twenty-eight children between the ages of four and fifteen. They had piled into a small truck and covered the children with tarps. They were within 200 meters of the crossing point when a German patrol appeared. Cohn, born in Mannheim, Germany, had joined the Movement de la Jeunesse Sioniste (Zionist Youth Movement) in 1942. She was intent on smuggling the Jewish children, whose parents had been expelled from France, into Switzerland.

Cohn and the twenty-eight children were imprisoned in the town of Annemasse. Cohn was beaten so badly she was unrecognizable. Meanwhile, Jean Deffaugt, the mayor of Annemasse, succeeded in convincing the Germans to release seventeen of the children temporarily. They sent Cohn and the remaining children, five boys and six girls, to the kitchen of the German command post, the Hôtel de France, to work each day. Underground workers began planning her rescue, hoping to spirit her away on a day when she was en route to the hotel. When told of the plan, she refused to abandon the children. During the night of July 3 or July 8, the Gestapo arrived from Lyon and disappeared with Cohn and two other women. Her body was found on August 21 when Annemasse was liberated. She was naked except for a blouse and a yellow pair of shoes. The blow of a spade had evidently killed her.

### BIBLIOGRAPHY

Latour, Anny. *The Jewish Resistance in France (1940–1944)*. Trans. Irene R. Ilton. New York: Holocaust Library, 1981; EncHol.

# COOK, IDA W., and COOK, LOUISE

(?–?)
Underground Workers, Great Britain

The Cook sisters, by traveling as tourists in the period prior to World War II, established a system for rescuing refugees. The two women were born in England. Their father was a customs official with a modest salary, and the two women learned to become independent soon after their

schooling ended. Louise entered the Civil Service and Ida became a typist. The two became obsessed with opera and often walked to save bus
money to buy tickets. Eventually, they were traveling to Europe and
New York to attend their favorite performances.

When the Nazi persecution began in Germany, they became aware of
the efforts of the refugee committee to help men, women, and children
escape from Nazi-occupied countries. They began to coordinate money
and shelter for a few individual cases on their trips to Europe. When
they had enough money, they contacted a friend or relative to sign the
official guarantee form. Louise learned to speak German, and Ida financed their work by writing romantic novels. She also handled the correspondence and written appeals. Every few months the two made a trip
to the continent to attend to their cases personally, sometimes only for
a weekend. They usually flew to Cologne, caught a train to Munich,
stopped off in Frankfurt where most of their cases were, and returned
by way of Holland. Clemens Krauss, head of the Munich Opera House,
had introduced the women to refugee work and provided them with full
details of opera performances in case authorities questioned them.

While in Germany they interviewed from ten to fifteen men or women
hoping to escape, decided whom to help, then, according to Ida's autobiography, *We Followed Our Stars* (1950), they retired to their hotel room
to cry. On their return trips to England, they wore jewelry and fur coats
smuggled out for the refugees against the time they escaped and would
need money. They established a clearinghouse for arriving refugees in
London and often had people living in their tiny flat. They quickly ex-
hausted their resources, but Ida began lecturing on "The Refugee Problem" and making appeals in church newspapers, and funds were
provided until their last journey into Germany in August 1939.

After war was declared in England, Ida and Louise Cook were separated. When London officials evacuated Louise's office to a remote location in Wales, their part in the war had ended.

## BIBLIOGRAPHY

Cook, Ida. *We Followed Our Stars*. New York: William Morrow, 1950; BioIn 2;
WrDr 84.

# D

## DAGOVER, LIL

(1897–1980)
Actress, Germany

Lil Dagover, a famous actress during the Third Reich, was born in Ma-diven, Java (now Djawa), on September 30, 1897. Her name was Maria Antonia Siegelinde Marta Liletts Seubert, but she eventually changed it to Lil Dagover. Her father was Ludwig Moritz Seubert, a forester and Dutch government employee. She was educated in Baden-Baden and began acting while at boarding school in Weimar. A fellow actor, Fritz Daghofer, introduced her to the director Robert Wiene, whom she even-tually married in 1917 and divorced in 1919. Wiene recommended her to Fritz Lang who cast her in her first film, *Harakiri (Madame Butterfly)* in 1919. Wiene later cast her in *The Cabinet of Dr. Caligari*, a film that became a classic. She became an international film and stage star work-ing in Austria, Switzerland, Luxembourg, Sweden, France, and the United States, as well as Germany. She became one of the most glam-orous stars of the 1930s.

During the Third Reich she continued to make films in Germany, but she was not seen in America or England until the 1970s. She won the coveted Staatsschauspieler (State Actress) title in 1939, probably for her roles in *Der Kongress Tanzt* (The Congress Dances; 1931), *Der Hohere Befehl* (The High Command; 1935), and *Die Kreutzersonate* (1936). In 1944 she was awarded the War Merit Cross. She also acted in the Deutsches Theater Berlin, the Salzburg Festival, and at war theatres. As with many other actresses, she was rumored to be a close friend of Adolf Hitler. She wrote her memoirs in 1979 and died the next year on January 23, 1980, in Munche-Geiselgasteig at age eighty-three.

**BIBLIOGRAPHY**

WhoWNG; EncWT; InWom; FilmgC 1; FilmgC 2; FilmgC; OxFilm; WhoHol; ConAu 105; AnnObit of 80.

# DELBO, CHARLOTTE

**(1913–1984)**
**Resistance Fighter, France**

Charlotte Delbo, who survived Auschwitz and Ravensbruck to write about her experiences, was born in Vigneux-sur-Seine, near Paris, in 1913. She worked as assistant to the theater impresario Louis Jouvet. In 1940 she was touring in South America with Jouvet's theatrical company when Hitler invaded France. When word came that the Gestapo had executed a friend, she insisted on returning to France in November 1941, despite Jouvet's strong opposition. Delbo entered the unoccupied zone of France by way of Portugal and Spain to join her husband, Georges Delbo, who was in the Resistance.

In March 1942 French police arrested Delbo and her husband for editing and producing anti-Nazi literature. Police turned them over to the Gestapo, who imprisoned them. Officials allowed Charlotte to visit her husband briefly before a firing squad executed him in May of that year. She was kept in France until the end of 1942 and sent to Auschwitz in January 1943, along with 230 French women, most of whom were also involved in underground activities. Only forty-nine of the women survived, and Delbo described each of them but one in her later writing. She was kept at Auschwitz and at Raisko, a satellite camp, until January 1944, when authorities moved her to Ravensbruck. She remained there until the end of the war when the Red Cross moved her to Sweden. When she returned home to France, she tracked down the two police officers who had arrested her and her husband and had them arrested. However, the courts found that the two had joined the Resistance and so they did not punish them.

Delbo described her experiences in a trilogy of books titled *Auschwitz and After*, which were published between 1946 and 1985, the year after her death.

### BIBLIOGRAPHY

Delbo, Charlotte. *Auschwitz and After*. Reprint. New Haven: Yale University Press, 1995.

## DIETRICH, MARLENE

(1901–1992)
**Actress, Anti-Nazi, Germany**

Marie Magdalene Dietrich was born on December 27, 1901, in Berlin, Germany. She was educated at the Augusta Victoria School in Berlin and at boarding schools in Weimar. During the 1920s, Dietrich found work as a chorus girl in a traveling revue in Germany. In 1922 she was accepted into Max Reinhardt's Deutsche Theaterschule and began appearing in minor roles in various films. She also had minor jobs playing the violin in an orchestra that accompanied silent films. She went to the United States to appear in films, but returned to Germany in 1934. She contributed a large amount of money to the German Film Organization's Welfare Fund, but two days later the Nazis banned her movie *Song of Songs* saying she painted Germany in a bad light because she had portrayed prostitutes in her movies. The Nazis began spreading rumors that she really wasn't German, and Hitler began screening her films in private for evidence against her. She returned to America and became an American citizen. The Nazis accused her of betraying her country and called her un-German.

When America entered the war in 1941, Dietrich became very active in selling war bonds. She sold them on radio and in person at rallies, on street corners, and across the country on four nationwide tours. She became the champion war bond salesperson, outselling all other movie stars. She received a Treasury Department citation for her efforts and would later be given the Medal of Freedom in 1947 for her efforts in entertaining the troops, and the Chevalier de la Legion d'Honneur in 1951.

Dietrich worked at the Hollywood Canteen every night for months and eventually began touring with a USO show, singing and playing the musical saw. She also performed a mental telepathy act which Orson Welles taught her. As part of the USO show she visited Greenland, the

Azores, Casablanca, Naples, England, Paris, Belgium, Holland, and many other cities and countries. Dietrich was the first Allied entertainer to perform in Anzio and Rome, and spent her forty-third birthday performing for the United States' Ninety-ninth Army near Bastogne, France, location of the Battle of the Bulge. She suffered from the cold and often had frostbite. She slept in sleeping bags in frozen fields and washed her hair and underclothes in the snow she melted in her helmet. She suffered from various bug infestations and pneumonia. In the winter of 1944–1945, Dietrich finally entered Germany where her family had remained. She found her sister Elisabeth and her brother-in-law had been living in Bergen-Belsen concentration camp, not as prisoners, but as members of a support group working with the Nazis. She denied her sister's existence when she found this out. She also located her mother in Berlin, but her mother died on November 6, 1945. After the war Dietrich declared that the war was the only important thing she had ever done in her life. She died on May 6, 1992. Dietrich was buried in Berlin with the medals she had earned from various nations for her work and performances during the war.

## BIBLIOGRAPHY

"Dietrich Returns." *New York Times Magazine*, September 22, 1946, 36–37; Bach, Steven. *Marlene Dietrich: Life and Legend*. New York: William Morrow and Company, 1992; AnnObit of 92; obituary in NewYT, May 7, 1992, A-1+; obituary in *Newsweek*, May 18, 1992, 72; obituary in *Time*, May 18, 1992, 72; obituary in *U.S. News & World Report*, May 18, 1992, 15; NewYTBE 72, 76; WhoAm 74, 76, 78, 80, 82; WhoAmW 74, 58, 64, 66, 68, 70, 72; WhoHol; WhoWor 74, 78, 82; WhoThe 77, 81; IntDcWB; IntWW 77–83; EncWT; FilmgC; BioIn 1–12; InWom.

# DODD, MARTHA STERN

(1908–1990)
**Author, Political Dissident, United States**

Martha Dodd, daughter of the American Ambassador to Germany from 1933 to 1937 and chronicler of the rise of Hitler in her memoir *Through Embassy Eyes* published in 1939, was born on October 8, 1908, in Ashland, Virginia. She attended the University of Chicago from 1926 to 1930 where she came under the influence of the works of Dostoevsky, Tolstoy, Chekhov, Nietzsche, and Robert Moss Lovett, a left-wing English professor. She was working as an assistant literary editor at the Chicago *Tribune* when her father, William Dodd, was named U.S. Ambassador to

Germany. She and her brother accompanied their parents to Berlin. In 1934 Putzi Hanfstaengl, an American who had access to Adolf Hitler and, as such, was trying to improve German–American relations, suggested that Dodd could change the destiny of Europe if she were to marry Hitler (*Newsweek*, August 26, 1957). When she met Hitler, however, she was disappointed. He kissed her hand politely then ignored her; she decided he was incapable of a relationship with a woman. Eventually she turned against Nazism after seeing the brutality, the concentration camps, and the effects on some of her friends.

Dodd's father resigned in 1938 and the family returned to the United States. Martha, however, decided to return to Germany, where she condemned Fascism and Hitler and proposed a United States alliance with Russia. Her name began to appear in subversive Communist groups. She married Alfred Stern, an American millionaire, in 1938, and when she was contacted by Soviet espionage to recruit new members, her conservative husband was one of her first recruits. After her father's death in 1941, she and her brother, William E. Dodd, Jr., edited *Ambassador Dodd's Diary: 1933–1938*. In 1944, Martha was the technical adviser for the Hollywood film adaptation of her book *Through Embassy Eyes*. The next year (1945) she wrote a novel called *Soaring the Wind* that described the disintegration of a German airman.

Meanwhile, the Sterns became more active in Soviet espionage activities and attracted the attention of the Federal Bureau of Investigation. Her specialty was atomic espionage and her task was to approach potential agents and couriers and see that they were introduced into actual espionage cells. She worked closely with Vassili Zubilin, wartime second secretary of the Soviet Embassy in Washington and head of the atomic espionage ring, and later Bill Browder, head of the U.S. Communist Party in charge of setting up a center in the United States and Mexico. Alfred Stern set up a dummy corporation in Mexico, and husband and wife traveled freely across the border on Soviet business.

After the war the Sterns became openly active in the Communist Party. In 1954 when a newspaper columnist hinted that Dodd was about to be subpoenaed by the McCarthy House Un-American Activities Committee and two of the spy cell, Jack and Myra Soble, were arrested and turned state's evidence, the Sterns prepared to flee back to Europe. The Sterns were subpoenaed to testify before the New York grand jury investigating Soviet espionage, agreed, and accepted $976 for transportation and witness fees. Meanwhile they sold $532,000 worth of securities and two weeks later fled to Zurich, then Prague where they disappeared.

**BIBLIOGRAPHY**

Alsterlund, B. "Martha Dodd." *Wilson Library Bulletin* 20 (February 1946): 394; "Ex-Ambassador's Daughter . . . a Red Spy." *Newsweek*, August 26, 1957, 23–30; "Travelers." *Time*, September 2, 1957, 17–18; CurBio 46; WhoAmJ 64; BioIn 1, 4; InWom; CurBioYrbk 91; obituary in NewYT, August 29, 1990, 22.

## DÖNHOFF, MARION

(1909–   )
**Underground Worker, Germany**

Marion Dönhoff was born in Friedrichstein, Germany, on December 2, 1909, into the aristocratic family of August and Maria Dönhoff. She attended the University of Frankfurt in Germany, the University of Basel in Switzerland, and Smith College in the United States. She returned to the family castle to help manage the estates when World War II broke out.

As she watched the fleeing refugees, she was struck by the fact that their carts lacked adequate protective covering or were so weighted down by heavy rugs that they could not take much baggage. She devised a method of making straw mats and built light wooden frameworks to use as "superstructures" on their wagons. A representative of the regional administrator appeared at her home after a Nazi informer reported her and they told her that if she continued preparing for flight, she would be punished. Despite their warnings she continued to help the refugees, organizing a "mobilization plan" that dictated which men from which estates would drive the carts and the maximum amount each family could take. She helped lead the refugees through a maze of country roads but eventually had to abandon her efforts and strike out on her own. She traveled on horseback for two months, often through snowstorms, and finally arrived in Hamburg. She joined the German underground and began regular, clandestine trips to Berlin where she played a role in many of the assassination attempts against Hitler.

After the war Dönhoff joined the editorial staff of *Die Zeit* and demanded all German criminals be punished. When Chancellor Konrad Adenauer appointed Theodor Oberlander to his Cabinet, Dönhoff pointed out his alleged involvement in the persecution of South Poland's

Jews during the war; eventually the minister was let go. She became editor of *Die Zeit* in 1968 and in 1971 won the German Book Publisher's Peace Prize.

## BIBLIOGRAPHY

Dönhoff, Marion. *Foe into Friend: The Makers of the New Germany.* Trans. Gabriele Annan. New York: St. Martin's Press, 1982; "Outspoken Gräfin." *Time,* September 13, 1963, 58; Dönhoff, Marion. *Before the Storm: Memoirs of My Youth in Old Prussia.* New York: Alfred A. Knopf, 1990; BioIn 6; IntAu&W 82; IntWW 80, 83.

# DRAENGER, TOVA

## (1917–1943?)
### Underground Leader, Poland

Tova Draenger was born in 1917 in Cracow, Poland. She became one of the leaders of the Akiva movement in Cracow in 1938 and with Shimshon Draenger edited the *Tse'irim* weekly reader for children. When the Nazis invaded Poland in 1939, she became one of the founders of an underground movement, He-Haluts ha-Lohem. On September 22, 1939, she and Shimshon Draenger were arrested, supposedly because they belonged to the Austrian anti-Nazi Irene Harand group. Authorities took them to Troppau, a Czechoslovakian prison camp, but released them in December. They reorganized Akiva in Cracow and Warsaw and were married that year. They continued their underground work. The authorities arrested Shimson Draenger again on January 18, 1943, and as they had agreed beforehand, Tova Draenger turned herself in to the Gestapo. She was taken to Montelupich prison, and while there she wrote her memoirs on toilet paper. Fellow cellmates helped her make several copies of the memoirs that covered the history of Akiva and He-Haluts ha-Lohem between April 1941 and March 1943. Fifteen of the twenty chapters survived and were eventually published under the title *Justina's Diary* (1978).

Draenger and her husband eventually escaped from prison in April 1943 and resumed their work with the underground in Wisnicz forest. They resumed publication of *He-Haluts ha-Lohem,* the underground organization's journal. In November 1943, her husband was arrested again and Draenger once again surrendered to the Gestapo. They both disappeared and were thought to have been killed.

## BIBLIOGRAPHY

Dawidson, G. *Justina's Diary.* Tel Aviv, 1978; EncHol.

Constance Drexel. New
York World-Telegram &
Sun collection, courtesy of
the Library of Congress.

## DREXEL, CONSTANCE

**(1894–1956)**
**Journalist, Germany**

Constance Drexel was born on November 28, 1894, to Theodore Drexel,
head of a wealthy Frankfurt family, and Zela Audeman Drexel, daughter
of a prominent Swiss watch manufacturer. The family moved to the
United States the following year and Drexel grew up in Roslindale, Massachusetts. She attended the Sorbonne in Paris and during World War I

was the first American woman to volunteer as a Red Cross nurse. In the summer of 1914 Drexel was stationed at a French hospital at Domville. She attended the International Woman's Congress at the Hague in April 1915, where she sent cable dispatches to the New York *Tribune*. Drexel also covered the Paris Peace Conference and wrote about the role of women in Czechoslovakia and Poland. In 1920 she was on the U.S. staff of the *Public Ledger* to cover the suffrage campaign and became the first woman political correspondent in Washington, D.C. For twenty years Drexel continued as a newspaper journalist and became an authority on international arms control and a champion of world peace.

As the world headed toward war, Drexel emerged as a proponent of Nazi philosophy. She approved of the role of German women in the Third Reich to produce more sons for the Reich and soon the Nazi Propaganda Ministry was giving her writing assignments. In 1939 she left for Germany, supposedly to care for an ailing mother in Wiesbaden. In 1940 she started broadcasting over the Reichrund Funk as "a famous American journalist," offering social and cultural commentaries. Her Sunday broadcasts featured the pleasures of life in wartime Germany with occasional political comments.

Drexel was arrested by American G.I.s on August 16, 1945. She spent a year in jail and internment camps before being exonerated by a Board of Inquiry. She arrived in New York City on October 2, 1946. On April 14, 1948, a treason indictment was dismissed and she continued her journalism career. She died on August 28, 1956, in Waterbury, Connecticut.

## BIBLIOGRAPHY

Edwards, John Carver. *Berlin Calling: American Broadcasters in Service to the Third Reich*. New York: Praeger, 1991, 15–21; Constance Drexel files, FBI, Department of Justice, Washington, D.C.; Ross, Ishbel. *Ladies of the Press: The Story of Women in Journalism by an Insider*. New York: Harper and Brothers, 1936, 514; Boughner, Genevieve J. *Women in Journalism*. New York: D. Appleton Century, 1942, 251–52; Rolo, Charles J. *Radio Goes to War*. New York: G. P. Putnam's Sons, 1942, 104; AnnObit of 79; BioIn 4; obituary in NewYT, August 29, 1956, 29.

# F

## FENELON, FANIA

(1918–1983)
**Musician, Camp Prisoner, France**

Fania Fenelon was born on September 2, 1918, in Paris to Jules Goldstein and Marie Bernier Goldstein. She graduated from the Paris Conservatory of Music in 1934 and became a successful music hall chanteuse. In 1940 she joined the Resistance. She was given the job of photographing the contents of briefcases carried by drunk German officers in cabarets. In 1943 she was arrested and tortured before being sent to Drancy, a detention house outside of Paris. On January 20, 1944, she was sent to Auschwitz. She was then taken to Birkenau concentration camp where a Polish guard was looking for someone who could sing Madame Butterfly. She volunteered and became a singer in the Auschwitz all-female orchestra. Although the "orchestra girls," as they were called, played for prisoners and SS officers and their wives, they did not receive extra rations and were hungry, dirty, and ragged.

Birkenau was liberated on April 15, 1945. Fenelon remained in Germany because she wanted to see the destruction and she joined a troupe of performers entertaining American G.I.s. Her memoir, *Playing for Time*, was published in 1976 and became a controversial television movie when British actress Vanessa Redgrave, a pro-Palestinian activist, was cast as Fenelon. Meanwhile, Fenelor resumed her career and performed all over

Fania Fenelon. AP/WIDE WORLD PHOTOS.

Europe; she always included a song she had learned at Auschwitz in her performances. Eventually Fenelon became a professor of music at conservatories in Dresden, Leipzig, and East Berlin. She died of cancer at Kremlin Bicetre Hospital in Paris in December 1983. She was at work on a new book about her experiences when she died.

### BIBLIOGRAPHY

"Musical Gift Meant Survival." NewYT, January 7, 1978, 42–43; obituary in NewYTBS, December 1983, 1439; ConAu 77–80; BioIn ll.

# FIOCCA, NANCY

(1916–   )
**Resistance Fighter, France**

Nancy Fiocca, a national heroine in France, was an Australian journalist whose marriage to French industrialist Henri Fiocca put her in Paris at the time of the war. She drove an ambulance until she and her husband were forced to flee to Marseilles. She joined the escape organization, Patronat. After two-and-a-half years in Marseilles, she decided to flee to Britain, but was arrested in Toulouse. The head of Patronat, Albert Guerisse, told police she was his mistress and had committed an "indiscretion." Fiocca was released and she continued to try to escape to Britain. Finally, after six tries, she arrived in Britain in June, 1943. She joined the Special Operations Executive (SOE), was trained in sabotage and returned to France to continue her resistance work with the Maquisards. She was part of a battle with 22,000 Germans on June 20, 1944, and participated in raids in Montlucon, where she was stationed, including one which destroyed Gestapo headquarters. As the war neared its end, she was hailed as a national heroine.

**BIBLIOGRAPHY**

WhoWWII.

# FLEISCHMANN, GISI

(1892–1944)
**Resistance Fighter, Rescuer, Slovakia**

Gisi Fleischmann, a Zionist activist in Slovakia, was born in Bratislava, Czechoslovakia, on January 21, 1892, to Julius (Judah) and Jetty Fischer, an Orthodox Jewish family. After her marriage to Josef Fleischman, she was drawn to Zionism. As rumors of war erupted in 1939, she sent her two children to Palestine and stayed behind to help the Jews. She traveled to Paris and London with Dr. Robert K. Fuered, head of the Central Jewish Relief Committee of Slovakia, and Dr. Y. O. Newman, president of the Slovakian Zionist Organization, to arouse the conscience of the world to Nazi victims, but considered the trip a failure. Fleischmann was head of the Women's International Zionist Organization in Slovakia and was a chief founder of the Procovna Skupina (Working Group), a group dedicated to rescuing Jews. She began corresponding with Jewish groups abroad and made several trips to Hungary to raise funds for the Jews of Slovakia and Poland. She also helped establish contact with the Jewish Agency office in Istanbul and the Heltalutz Center in Geneva. She was part of the group that tried to bribe Adolf Eichmann's representative in Slovakia, Dieter Wisliceny, to stop deportation of Slovakian Jews. She was also part of the group that came up with the Europa Plan, another attempt to save Jews through negotiation and money.

Although Fleischmann often felt her political attempts at saving Jews were failures, she did manage to aid them at other times. In 1940 she helped 326 Jews from Prague whom the Nazis had interned in a camp in Cessnock, Poland. She convinced the Slovak government to allow them to remain while she found a safe place for them. With Richard Lichtheim, the Jewish Agency representative in Geneva, and Henry Monter, the representative of the United Palestine Appeal in New York, she found a safe place and most reached Palestine before deportations began in 1942.

Fleischmann was especially concerned in getting as many children to safety as possible and at one time, she and her colleagues had twenty houses full of rescued children in Budapest. In 1943, when Dieter Wisliceny proposed to send thousands of children to Palestine by way of Rumania, she campaigned strenuously for their safety. The plan failed at the last minute when the "fanatically anti-Jewish" Haj Am el Husaini, Grand Mufti of Jerusalem, lodged a sharp protest with Heinrich Himmler. The children were sent to Auschwitz where they died.

As conditions in Slovakia worsened, Fleischmann continued to negotiate to exchange money for the release of Jews. Her friends and the Jewish Council advised everyone who could to escape, but Fleischmann refused to leave. She continued negotiating with the wife of Isidor Koso, head of the president's chancellery, to aid the Jews in exchange for Koso's son attending a private school in Switzerland. She wrote a letter of introduction to friends in Switzerland for Mrs. Koso and was arrested shortly after that and placed in solitary confinement. She was released but rounded up again on September 28, 1944, along with 1,800 others. She was left behind to liquidate the affairs of the Jewish Council and was arrested again in October 1944. This time she was sent to Auschwitz as a "return undesirable" because of her highly visible rescue activities and was gassed on arrival.

## BIBLIOGRAPHY

Campion, Joan. *In the Lion's Mouth: Gisi Fleischmann and the Jewish Fight for Survival*. Lanham, Md.: University Press of America, 1987; Neumann, Y. O. *Gisi Fleischmann: The Story of a Heroic Woman*. Tel Aviv: World Wizo Executive, 1970; Varon, Benno Weiser. "Gisi Fleischmann's 'Non-Commercial' Sacrifice." *Boston Jewish Times*, December 8, 1983, 2; EncHol.

# FOURCADE, MARIE-MADELEINE

(1909–1989)
**Resistance Fighter, France**

Marie-Madeleine Fourcade was born on November 8, 1909, in Marseilles, France. In 1937 in Paris, Marie Fourcade was the general secretary of a magazine publishing group and was running a journal, *L'Ordre National*, almost single-handedly because of the mobilization of troops. When the paper closed down in September 1939, she fled to Paris. She joined a Légion des Combattants group in Vichy in September and was given the job of organizing the underground. She was to divide the unoccupied zone into sectors designed to observe the enemy and disperse couriers in every direction. She eventually made her headquarters in Pau at the Hôtel de Lycée and led "the life of a prisoner," never going out by day and rarely by night as she ran her side of the organization. When her mother was arrested, Fourcade fled by train, hidden in a mail bag. She was in the mail bag for nine hours wearing minimal clothing in freezing temperatures.

In 1942 she returned to Vichy and helped set up a new organization known as Noah's Ark, giving every agent an animal's name. (She was "Hedgehog.") She was imprisoned in l'Eveche in Marseilles in November and interrogated by the Nazis. On November 11, 1942, the Germans invaded the city and they released her. Meanwhile, the organization had swelled from about a hundred to nearly a thousand. Fourade's mother was imprisoned and then released, but the Germans demanded that the Jesuits at her son's school give the boy up as a hostage. The Jesuits refused, and her mother was able to smuggle the child out and place him in a center for Jewish children run by a Christian organization. Her daughter was later placed in the same center, and then both children were smuggled out to Switzerland. Her cover blown again, Fourcade managed to get to Paris and eventually to England, and Noah's Ark was destroyed.

In 1944 she returned to Aix but was picked up by the Gestapo and placed in the prison on Rue Rifle-Rafle. Fourcade managed to squeeze through the bars of a window by taking off all her clothes. She was rescued and taken back to Marseilles, then Verdun, where she was in regular contact with Gen. George S. Patton's headquarters. She made frequent trips between the eastern front and Paris until the end of the war. In 1968 she published an account of the organization known as Noah's Ark in *L'Arche de Nöe* (published in English in 1973). As a member of the Committee for the Defence of Human Rights and of the League Against Racism and Anti-Semitism, she was a witness at the trial of Klaus Barbie in 1987. She was working to rescue refugees from Lebanon weeks before her death at age 79.

### BIBLIOGRAPHY

Fourcade, Marie-Madeleine. *Noah's Ark*. London: George Allen & Unwin Ltd., 1973; Vlansson-Ponte, Pierre. *King and His Court*. Boston: Houghton Mifflin, 1964; WhoF 79; BioIn 17; AnnObit of 89.

## FRANK, ANNE

**(1929–1945)**
**Author, Hidden Child, Germany**

Anne Frank, who became known for her diary while in hiding from the Nazis, was born in Frankfurt, Germany, on June 12, 1929, to Otto Heinrich Frank, a businessman, and Edith Hollander Frank. The Franks moved to Amsterdam in 1933 because of rising anti-Semitism. Anne's father was director of Travies N.V. and a partner in Kolen & Co., both housed in the same building. Anne learned to speak Dutch and attended a Montessori school in Amsterdam. On May 10, 1940, the Germans invaded and occupied the Netherlands, and once again the Frank family was confronted with anti-Jewish rules and laws. Anne was forced to switch to the Jewish Lyceum because Jewish children could only attend Jewish schools. Meanwhile, Otto Frank began preparing a hiding place for his wife and Anne, and her sister Margot, who was three years older. He chose a vacant annex to his office at Prinsengracht 263. He was aided in his preparations by four close employees, Victor Kugler, Johannes Kleiman, Elli Voskuijl, and Miep Gies.

On July 5, 1942, Anne's sister Margot received a registered letter from the Zentralstelle für Judische Auswanderung (Central Office for Jewish Emigration). It ordered her to register at the bureau. At this point, Frank moved his family into their hiding place. A week later the van Daan family, including fifteen-year-old Peter, also moved in. On November 16, 1942, an eighth member of the group was added when a dentist by the name of Friedrich Pfeffer joined them. The eight of them spent two years in the tiny annex while Frank's employees foraged for food and clothing for them. Then on August 4, 1944, the SD (*Sicherheitsdienst* or Security Service) in Amsterdam received an anonymous phone call that the group was hiding at Prinsengracht 263. All eight were found and arrested. Many papers were scattered on the floor and among them was the diary that Anne had kept during her two years of hiding. The Franks were transported to Westerbork transit camp on August 8, 1944, then to Auschwitz on September 3. Edith Frank, Anne, and Margot were taken to Frauenblock, and Edith died on January 6, 1945, at Auschwitz-Birkenau. Anne and Margot were sent to Bergen-Belsen at the end of October 1944. A typhus epidemic struck the camp, and Margot died of typhus sometime in March 1945. Anne died two days later. Otto Frank was the only one of the group to survive. He was in the hospital at Auschwitz when the camp was liberated on January 27, 1945.

Anne's diary was published in 1947 in Dutch, in 1952 in English, and eventually became a movie in 1959. It has been the basis for two Broadway shows, in 1955 and then in 1997.

## BIBLIOGRAPHY

Galen, Last, D. van. *Anne Frank and After*. Amsterdam: Amsterdam University Press, 1996; Frank, Anne. *Diary of a Young Girl*. Trans. B. M. Mooyaart. New York: Doubleday, 1952; Steenmeiser, Anna G., ed. *Tribute to Anne Frank; In Collaboration with Otto Frank and Henri Van Praag*. New York: Doubleday, 1970; Lindwer, Willy. *Anne Frank*. English. Trans. Alison Meersschaert. New York: Pantheon Books, 1991; Graver, Lawrence. *An Obsession with Anne Frank: Meyer Levin and The Diary*. Berkeley: University of California Press, 1995; Meinick, Ralph. *The Stolen Legacy of Anne Frank: Meyer Levin, Lillian Hellman, and the Staging of The Diary*. New Haven, CT: Yale University Press, 1997; TwCW; BioIn 2, 3, 4, 5, 7, 8, 10, 11, 12; EncTR; HerW; InWom; LinLibL; WhoWWII; IntDcWB.

# FRIANG, ELIZABETH

(1924–   )
**Resistance Fighter, France**

Elizabeth Friang was born on January 23, 1924, and sixteen short years later was involved in student protests in Paris. Authorities expelled her from the Lycée for writing BBC messages from Charles de Gaulle on the blackboard during lunch breaks. She engraved a Lorraine Cross and a "V" for Victory on the school window. Friang then began stealing weapons from German soldiers on the Metro or restaurant cloakrooms and slashed German propaganda posters. In September 1943, the Commander of the Resistance network, Jean-François Clouet des Perushes (code name "Galilee"), contacted Elizabeth and she became his assistant with the code name of "Brigitte." She continued to live at home with her family and kept her radio equipment under her bed. She spent nights coding and decoding messages from England. She recruited other agents and organized the drops of arms and men.

Friang continued her activities until March 21, 1944, when she was assigned to rescue an agent at Gestapo headquarters. When she arrived at her meeting place at the Trocadero Aquarium, she was surrounded by Gestapo agents. She struck one in the solar plexus and ran. She was shot three times; one bullet entered her lower back and exited through her stomach. She was put in a car and tried to fall out, hoping she would die, but an agent hit her on the jaw. When she was on the operating table the Gestapo continued questioning and hitting her. The German doctors, furious, left the nurses to put on emergency bandages and the questioning continued. They refused to give her painkillers and broke her teeth and jaw. She was taken to Fresnes prison where the interrogation continued for seven weeks. On May 10, 1944, she was sent to Ravensbruck, then to Zwodau concentration camp in Czechoslovakia. Meanwhile, she had developed tuberculosis. A camp doctor saved her by telling the SS she had a contagious disease.

As the Soviets advanced on the camp, 1,700 internees were taken on a forced, three-week, 450-mile march. At the end, only 200 internees, including Friang, were alive. She escaped on May 8, 1944, and found American troops who sent her home to Paris.

Friang continued to be involved in wartime activities even after World War II. She was a war correspondent in Indochina from 1951 to 1970, the first and, for a long time, the only woman.

Elizabeth (Brigitte) Friang. AP/WIDE WORLD PHOTOS.

## BIBLIOGRAPHY

Saywell, Shelley. "Le Resau: France, 1939–45." *Women in War* (37–73). New York: Viking Penguin Inc., 1985; "Madame Parachute." *Newsweek*, May 31, 1954, 76; Au&Wr 71; BioIn 3; WhoF 79.

# G

## GETTER, MATYLDA

(?–1968)
**Rescuer, Poland**

Matylda Getter was Mother Superior of the Warsaw branch of the Order of Franciscan Sisters of the Family of Mary when World War II began. She worked as a teacher, mostly with orphaned children, and cared for the sick and elderly though she herself was ill with cancer. In 1942 she began helping Jewish children from the Warsaw Ghetto, sheltering as many as possible in various locations. She rescued an estimated several hundred Jewish children despite criticism that she had endangered non-Jewish children by doing so. She removed the Jewish children to other shelters when she believed a Gestapo raid was imminent. She often disguised them by wrapping their faces in bandages. Getter died in 1968 and was recognized by Yad Vashem as one of the "Righteous Among Nations."

### BIBLIOGRAPHY

Bartoszewski, W., and Z. Lewinowna, eds. *Righteous Among Nations: How Poles Helped the Jews, 1939–1945*. London: Earlscourt Publications, 1969; EncHol.

Matylda Getter. Yad Vashem Photo Archives,
courtesy of USHMM Photo Archives.

## GIEHSE, THERESE

**(1898–1975)**
**Actress, Germany**

Therese Giehse was a well-known actress at the outbreak of World War
II. In 1926 she was playing at the famous Munich Kammerspiel and had
been lauded as a "genuine German woman on the Jewish stage." She
began writing and singing satirical songs lampooning the Nazis at Die
Pfeffermühle (The Pepper Mill), a local cabaret, when the Nazis discovered she was of Bavarian–Jewish descent. Her life was in danger and she
fled to Zurich where she continued singing her satirical songs. The Nazis
labeled her a subversive agitator. Regardless, she continued acting at the
Zurich Schauspielhaus and returned to Germany after the war. She died
on March 11, 1975.

BIBLIOGRAPHY

EncTR; EncWT; WhoHol; AnnObit of 75.

# GILLARS, MILDRED ELIZABETH

(1901–1988)
Nazi Propagandist, United States

Mildred Elizabeth Gillars, who was tried for broadcasting Nazi propaganda during World War II, was born in Portland, Maine, on November 29, 1901. She attended Ohio Wesleyan College, where she was the first woman to wear knickers in the 1920s. She dropped out and tried to find work as an actress, first in Cleveland and then in New York. On September 4, 1934, she arrived in Berlin and taught English at the Berlitz Language School. She became involved with Dr. Max Otto Koischwitz, a former professor of German Literature at Hunter College in New York, who was working for German radio. Koischwitz developed two radio programs for Gillars entitled "Home Sweet Home" and "Midge at the Mike." Under her radio name of "Axis Sally," she broadcast propaganda messages to American troops in the European theater until 1945. Other of her radio nicknames were "Berlin Bait" and "Berlin Bitch." She played popular tunes and in between taunted Allied soldiers about their wives and girlfriends back home and described what would happen to the soldiers in battle.

When Germany fell to the Allies, Gillars lived for ten months in cellars before members of the U.S. Counter-Intelligence Corps discovered her in March 1946. Her blond hair had turned gray and she had eighteen cents in her pockets. They detained her for nine months near Frankfurt and released her on Christmas Eve. She was rearrested and the U.S. Justice Department announced on March 18, 1948, that it would prosecute her. The charges stemmed from the fact that she had taken part in radio programs after the Normandy Invasion and recorded interviews with wounded Americans in German prisons under the guise of a Red Cross worker who would send their messages to the United States. On September 10, 1948, she was indicted on ten counts of treason. A second trial before the U.S. District Court in Washington, D.C., began on January 24, 1949. Her lawyer used as her defense that (1) her broadcasts were not treasonous; and (2) she was coerced by Koischwitz into making them or she would have been imprisoned or killed if she refused. Gillars was found innocent on seven counts, but was convicted for the part she took in the "Vision of Invasion" broadcast twenty-five days before D-Day, in which she played an American mother who dreamed her G.I. son was killed during the cross-channel invasion. She was sentenced to thirty years in the Federal Reformatory for Women in Alderson, West Virginia, the same prison where Iva Ikuki Toguri D'Aquino, one of the women known in the Pacific as "Tokyo Rose," was jailed. A social service nun converted her to Catholicism while in prison.

Gillars was paroled in 1961 at age sixty and taught at a girls boarding school at the Sisters of the Poor Child Jesus Convent in Columbus, Ohio. In 1973 she returned to Ohio Wesleyan, where she obtained a bachelor's degree in speech at age seventy-two. She died of colon cancer at age eighty-seven.

### BIBLIOGRAPHY

"Kiss Me No More." *Newsweek*, July 17, 1961, 24+; "Newsmakers." *Newsweek*, June 25, 1973, 45; "People." *Time*, June 25, 1973, 52; "Big Role." *Time*, February 7, 1949, 15; "New Part for Sally." *Newsweek*, February 7, 1949, 20–21; Rovere, R. H. "Letter from Washington." *New Yorker*, February 26, 1949, 77–82; "Sally and Rose." *Time*, August 30, 1948, 13; "Shock for Sally." *Newsweek*, March 21, 1949, 31–32; EncTr; BioIn 1, 6, 8, 9; AnnObit of 88.

## GLAZER, GESJA

**(?–1944)**
**Underground Fighter, Lithuania**

Gesja Glazer, an underground fighter in Lithuania, was first known as an active member of the Communist Party, often imprisoned in jails and concentration camps. On June 22, 1941, Germany invaded the Soviet Union and Glazer fled deeper into the Soviet interior. From there, she dropped into Lithuania by parachute to set up an underground and partisan group. She entered the Kovno Ghetto as a representative of the Communist Party. She was then placed in charge of the fighting units of the Jewish underground in the Augustow forest. She kept in touch with the ghetto from the forest until February 1944, when she became active in the Vilna underground. When German police came to arrest her, she committed suicide.

### BIBLIOGRAPHY

EncHol.

# GLOEDEN, ELIZABETH CHARLOTTE LILO

(1903–1944)
**Resistance Worker, Germany**

Elizabeth Charlotte Lilo Gloeden, who was beheaded for sheltering a German army officer accused of treason, was born in Cologne, Germany, on December 19, 1903. In 1938 she married architect Erich Gloeden and the two settled in Berlin where they became active opponents of the Nazis. They sheltered many persecuted Germans including Dr. Carl Friedrich Goerdeler, the civilian leader of the Resistance. After the July 20, 1944, plot to kill Hitler, they sheltered Gen. Fritz Lindemain, who had been involved in the plot. The Gestapo offered a reward of 500,000 marks for Lindemain's arrest. The Gloedens managed to hide him for six weeks, but on September 3, 1944, the Gestapo arrested the entire family, including Lilo's mother. On November 30, 1944, the Germans beheaded Gloeden, her mother, and her husband at two minute intervals at Plotzensee Prison, an event publicized by the Nazis as a warning against hiding traitors.

**BIBLIOGRAPHY**

EncTR.

# GLUCK, GEMMA LA GUARDIA

(1881–1962)
**Political Prisoner, United States**

Gemma Gluck was born in an immigrant neighborhood in New York in 1881. Her father eventually became bandmaster for the United States Army, and the family lived in the Dakota Territory and Fort Huachuca and Prescott, both in Arizona. Her father was commissioned out of the Army after eating a can of tainted meat, and the family moved back to Trieste in 1901. Her father opened a tourist hotel and her brother, Fiorello La Guardia, returned to New York, was elected to Congress, and became mayor of New York City in 1933.

Gemma's Gluck's mother came from one of Italy's most prominent Jewish families, the Luzzati. Gemma married Herman Gluck, a Jew. When the Nazis came to power, the Glucks were living in Budapest, and Herman Gluck lost his job as an accountant in a bank because he was Jewish.

On April 19, 1944, Fiorello La Guardia made an appearance on the steps of New York's City Hall at a mass demonstration commemorating the first anniversary of the uprising in the Warsaw ghetto. He warned listeners that the Nazis would pay for their crimes and predicted their downfall. On May 12, SS officers ordered Hungarian detectives to search Gluck's house. For three hours they looked for the transmitter they thought she was using to communicate with her brother in New York. On June 7, 1944, Gemma Gluck and her husband were arrested. When asked why, they told her it was because she was La Guardia's sister. Nazi newspapers asked how Hungarians could permit the sister of La Guardia, "Hitler's greatest enemy," to continue to live in Budapest.

Gluck was placed in a second-class compartment on a train because of her status and taken to Mathausen prison in Vienna. There she was told that they were going to bring La Guardia to Berlin and hang him while she watched. On June 29, she was transferred to Ravensbruck where she became prisoner no. 44,139 and identified as a *Sonder-Hafling*, a special prisoner. She was placed in charge of a table of thirty-four women who called her "Mutti," or mother. She gave lessons in English in secret. In August, Gluck's daughter Yolanda and her five-month-old son arrived at Ravensbruck. The Germans brought them together on April 15, 1945, and told the family that they were being taken to Berlin as hostages to be exchanged for other prisoners. When the Russians entered Berlin, the Glucks were freed, but they knew no one in Berlin and had no money. As bombs fell overhead, they remained in an air-raid shelter at the train station for eleven days. A stranger then took them in and war correspondents got word of her whereabouts. They broadcast the news over the Mutual Broadcasting Company and La Guardia discovered they were alive. They, in turn, learned that Gemma's husband died at Mathausen and that her daughter's husband died of starvation. They went to Copenhagen on July 1, 1946, where they waited for visas for three months. Gluck arrived in New York on May 19, 1947, and her brother died on September 20. She ended her life in a small apartment in a municipal housing project built during her brother's administration. She died of a heart attack on November 2, 1962.

### BIBLIOGRAPHY

Gluck, Gemma La Guardia. *My Story*, edited by S. L. Shneiderman. New York: David McKay Company, 1961; obituary in NewYT, November 3, 1962, 25; BioIn 6.

# GOEBBELS, MAGDA

(1901–1945)
**Socialite, Nazi, Germany**

Magda Goebbels, the woman whom author Hans-Otto Meissner called the "First Lady of the Third Reich," was born on November 11, 1901, in Berlin. She was convent educated, spoke several languages, and was brought up in the best society. In 1930 she divorced her first husband, millionaire Gunter Quandt, and became engaged to Joseph Goebbels, a member of the NSDAP (National Socialist German Workers' Party). She saw him speak at a meeting in Berlin and joined the NSDAP a few days later. She read Adolf Hitler's *Mein Kampf*, studied the NS newssheet training instructions, followed Hitler's speeches in the press, and took over the leadership of the West End Women's Organization. She became Goebbels's secretary, in charge of managing his private archives. They married on December 12, 1931, with the approval of top Nazi officials, who added the ex-wife of one of Germany's wealthiest industrial magnates to their list of women who would bring social acceptance to the Nazi Party.

The Goebbels's home became the private headquarters of the party leadership and a sanctuary for Hitler when he was in Berlin. After an attempt was made to poison Hitler in January 1933, Magda and her trusted cook took charge of preparing Hitler's meals. Goebbels became Minister of Information and Propaganda, and Magda continued to bear children, six in all. Goebbels, for his part, was a noted philanderer, sometimes carrying on liaisons in the bedroom next to hers. In 1938 Magda approached Hitler about a divorce after months of collecting evidence of his many infidelities. Hitler asked her to wait one year and remain outwardly happily married. When the year was up, she signed a reconciliation agreement in August 1939. The agreement stipulated that a list of people would be drawn up who were no longer welcome in the Goebbels's home, including thirty women from the original list Magda had given Hitler a year earlier, and Goebbels's mistress, Lisa Baarova, who was never to enter Germany again. Friends who had remained loyal to Magda were not to be persecuted, while the men who had helped Goebbels in his affairs were to be transferred to remote units. Finally, Magda had the right to divorce Goebbels at any time and would keep the house, the children, and a substantial income. However, nothing changed. Goebbels continued his affairs, and Magda produced another child.

Meanwhile, the war was escalating and the Goebbels outfitted their residence behind the Wilhelmstrasse with a bomb shelter fourteen meters deep. It included paneled walls hung with artwork, thick carpets, bath, kitchen, and wine cellar. In March 1945, Magda told her ex-sister-in-law, Ello Quandt, of her plans to kill herself and the children even though her former husband, with whom she had remained close, offered to take the children to safety in Switzerland. She said she felt responsible for the suffering of others and did not want the children living in the shadow of Goebbels, one of the great criminals in the world. She followed the Buddhist belief that they would all be together in an afterlife.

On April 23, 1945, the Goebbels family moved to Hitler's bunker beneath the Reich Chancellery. On April 30, Hitler shook hands with Magda for the last time, then removed the gold Nazi Party badge from his coat and fastened it to Magda's jacket—for her the highest honor any woman could receive. The next day the Goebbels poisoned their six children and then emerged from the bunker where Joseph Goebbels shot himself and Magda swallowed poison.

### BIBLIOGRAPHY

Meissner, Hans-Otto. *Magda Goebbels: The First Lady of the Third Reich*. New York: Dial Press, 1980.

## GOERING, EMMY

**(1893–1973)**
**Actress, Nazi, Germany**

Before her marriage to Hermann Goering, the Nazi Luftwaffe commander, Emmy Sonneman was a well-known actress at the National Theater in Weimar. She was born in Hamburg, Germany, on March 24, 1893. She played leading roles in provincial theaters for several years before becoming a *Staatsschaupielerin* (state actress) in 1934. She was best known for the female lead in *Schlageter* by Hans Jonst. During this time, it was rumored that she and the theater's artistic director, Guston Grundgens, protected fellow artists who were Jewish.

Emmy divorced her first husband, actor Karl Köstlin, and married Goering on April 10, 1935, in a "quasi-royal" wedding in which Adolf Hitler served as best man. The birth of her daughter in 1937 was a national event; they named her Edda after Benito Mussolini's daughter.

After the war, Hermann Goering was sentenced to death for war crimes, but committed suicide by taking poison. In 1948 Emmy was con-

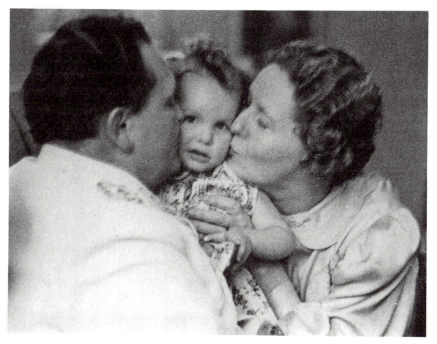

Emmy Goering. Goering collection, courtesy of the Library of Congress.

victed of being a Nazi in a German denazification trial in Garmisch-Partenkirchen. In spite of her repeated disavowals—that Kathleen McLaughlin of the *New York Times* called "the greatest performance of her career" (NewYTBS '73)—she was sentenced to a year in labor camp. The courts suspended her sentence because she had served fourteen months in confinement. She was released and 30 percent of her property was confiscated. Emmy Goering was barred from the stage for five years, but found she was unable to revive her career. She died on June 8, 1973, in Munich, in the small apartment she was still sharing with her daughter.

## BIBLIOGRAPHY

Irving, David John Cawdell. *Goering: A Biography*. London: Macmillan Publishers Ltd., 1989; NewYTBS '73; AnnObit of 79; EncTR; WhoWNG.

# GRANVILLE, CHRISTINE

**(1915–1952)**
**British Spy, Poland**

Krystyna Skarben, who, under the name of Christine Granville, was one of the most effective spies during the Third Reich, was born in 1915 to Count Jerzy Skarbek, a Polish aristocrat, and Stephanie Goldfeder Skarben, daughter of a Jewish banker. Skarben learned to shoot and ride and spoke French, German, and Russian in addition to her native Polish. She was living in Africa with her husband, George Gizycki, when Poland was invaded and Gizycki was killed. She went immediately to London and offered to go to Budapest to produce propaganda leaflets, organize the infiltration of POWs to Allied territories, and collect information. She was placed under the SOE (Special Operations Executive) and given the code name of "Christine Granville."

On December 31, 1939, she arrived in Budapest. She convinced Jan Marusarz, a ski-teacher and member of the Polish Olympic Team, to take her into Poland and the two left in February. They made their way through a blizzard in the Tatra mountains, in which thirty people died, to Warsaw and after five weeks of gathering information, returned over the mountains. In June 1940, Granville and Marusarz made a second trip to collect military and economic information. After her return to Budapest, Granville's mother was arrested and she never saw her again. In November she left Budapest to rescue sixteen British soldiers who had escaped from POW camps in Germany and were hiding in an asylum for the hearing impaired in Warsaw. Officials were afraid that the British soldiers were in danger because Adolf Hitler was about to carry out the extermination of the mentally and physically disabled. When Granville arrived, the soldiers had already left, but she was able to help two other soldiers escape. She took the men to Warsaw, left them in the care of a resistance group, and returned to Budapest to deliver vital information. When she arrived at the end of November, she had influenza, was suffering from exhaustion, and was coughing up blood. She was bedridden for two weeks.

In February 1941, Granville was arrested along with a co-worker, Andrew Kowerski, and interrogated. Granville bit her tongue to produce blood and began spitting the blood out, imitating the symptom of tuberculosis. X rays were ordered and they showed shadows on her lungs, possibly from poisoning by exhaust gas. The doctor mistook the shadows for tuberculosis and was instrumental in getting Granville and Kowerski released. The two went to the British Embassy and assumed new names. They reestablished contact with an organization in Poland and made arrangements for new routes for couriers before setting out for Turkey to carry microfilm from the Polish underground. The film showed hundreds of German trains, regiments, and ammunition on the Russian border. In Bulgaria she handed the microfilm over to the British, then made her way to Syria and the Turkish border in October 1941. She carried out reconnaissance of the bridges of the Tigris and Euphrates rivers.

For three years, Granville continued carrying out assignments. On July 6, 1944, under the new code name of "Jacqueline Armand," she parachuted into Vercors at Vassieux, in France. She was blown four miles off course, the butt of her revolver was broken, and she suffered a badly bruised coccyx. She joined an agent known only as "Roger," and their job was to organize groups of fifteen to twenty underground workers who were to be in charge of obtaining materials, including explosives and weapons. She recruited many Italians who had turned against the Germans and helped prepare for the Allied landings in the south of France. When the fighting became fierce at the Battle of Vercors, she left for Italy to meet 200 partisans in the Italian Alps, and then made her way to a mostly Polish garrison in a fort held by the Germans at Col de Larche, a mountain pass. She spoke to the Polish soldiers through a loudspeaker and convinced them to desert and join the Resistance. They were able to blow up the road and keep the Germans from attacking until the Americans could arrive.

For her efforts against the Nazis, Granville received many honors, including the George Medal on January 1, 1945, for saving the lives of the two British soldiers and the Croix de Guerre, avec etoile d'Argent, for saving a French officer. Other awards included the Order of the British Empire and the "Chamois" of the Association Nationale des Pionniers et Combattants Volontaires du Vercors. On November 31, 1944, she received an honorary commission in the Women's Auxiliary Air Force and was given an RAF uniform. She relinquished the commission on May 11, 1945, and returned to civilian life.

Civilian life was not kind to Granville. She had trouble finding a job and went to the south of France to aid an aging, poverty-stricken aunt. Back in London she experienced passport troubles and worked in several menial jobs while waiting to get a new passport. In 1947 she was working in the linen room in a hotel in Paddington when she finally received her passport. In 1950 she was honored at Vercors for her work during the war, but when she returned to London she was hit by a car and suffered a severe depression. She finally obtained a position as a stewardess for the Shaw Savill Line that ran between Australia and New Zealand. On board ship she met a man named Dennis George Muldowney, who became obsessed with her and began stalking her. She decided to abandon her room at the Shelbourne Hotel in Lexham Gardens in London and move where he would be unable to find her. On June 13, 1952, Muldowney confronted her as she was preparing to leave the hotel. Two days later Muldowney stabbed her in the breast and she died in the hallway of the hotel. Muldowney was hanged on September 30, 1952. On the way to the gallows he said, "To kill is the final possession."

**BIBLIOGRAPHY**

Seth, Ronald. *Some of My Favorite Spies*. Philadelphia: Chilton Book Company, 1968; Masson, Madeleine. *Christine: A Search for Christine Granville*. London: Hamish Hamilton, 1975; Laska, Vera, ed. *Women in the Resistance and in the Holocaust: The Voices of Eyewitnesses*. Westport, Conn.: Greenwood Press, 1988; "Countess." *Time*, June 30, 1952, 264; "Who Was Christine Granville?" *Life*, July 7, 1952, 43–45; BioIn 2, 3, 8, 9, 10; InWom; EncE 75.

# GRESE, IRMA

(1921–1946)
**Prison Camp Warden, Nazi, Germany**

Irma Grese, known variously as the Belle of Auschwitz, Angel of Death, Blonde Angel of Death, Blonde Angel of Hell, or the Beastess of Belsen, was born in 1921 in the small village of Wrecken in Germany. Her father refused to let Irma and her younger sister, Helena, join the girls' section of Hitler Youth until it became compulsory in 1936. Grese left school at age fourteen to work as a shop assistant in the nearby town of Lychen. In 1939 she became a probationer nurse at the famous sanatorium, Hohenlychen. At Hohenlychen she was influenced by Professor Karl Gebhardt, head of the hospital and influential in the Nazi regime (later hanged by the Americans in 1948). She became a fanatic Nazi but lost her job despite her fervor. The German Labor Exchange sent her to work in a dairy where she stayed for one year before joining the staff of the Ravensbruck concentration camp.

In 1942 or 1943 Grese was transferred to Auschwitz and put in charge of 18,000 (sometimes estimated as high as 30,000) female prisoners. During this time when she went home on leave, proudly wearing her SS uniform, her father beat her and turned her out of the house. According to reports, she often beat the prisoners with whips and rubber hoses, watched medical experiments, and selected prisoners for the gas chambers. She was rumored to have had affairs with Josef Kramer, camp commandant, and Dr. Josef Mengele, head camp physician.

In January 1945, camp authorities sent Grese with an evacuation convoy back to Ravensbruck where she remained for two months. In March she was placed in charge of another evacuation convoy to Bergen-Belsen. When the Allied liberators arrived on April 5, 1945, they arrested her. She was tried as a war criminal with forty-three other Belsen guards and on September 17, 1945, she was condemned to death. On December 10, 1945, she ate a special meal of sausage, rolls, and real coffee at the prison in Hamelin, Germany. She spent the night singing Nazi patriotic songs, then went screaming to the gallows where she was hanged at dawn.

### BIBLIOGRAPHY

Lustgarten, Edgar. "Irma Grese." In *This Business of Murder*. London: Harrap, 1966, 77–105; Ewart, Andrew. "Irma Grese." In *World's Wickedest Women*. New York: Taplinger, 1965, 262–78; EncTR; BioIn 7; InWom.

## GROSSMAN, HAIKA

**(1919– )**
**Underground Worker, Poland**

Haika Grossman, known for her underground work against the Germans in Bialystok, Poland, was born in that city in 1919. She became a member of the Zionist youth movement Ha-Shomer ha-Tsa'ir and was an organizer of the underground against the Nazis as early as 1941. Posing as an Aryan, she moved between underground units in Vilna, Warsaw, and other cities as a member of the "anti-Fascist Bialystok" cell. She became known for her daring, once traveling without papers on a train car reserved for German soldiers and often carrying a weapon across the city for delivery inside the ghetto. When she was sent to get Kuba Rogozinski, a movement veteran, and his wife, Naomi, out of Volkovisk concentration camp, Grossman went straight to the gates of the camp and told the guard one of the Jews inside had the keys to her storehouse. She managed to pass information to Kuba and get the two to comparative freedom. She was entrusted with establishing a communications center between Vilna and Warsaw and helped organize the fighting center in Bialystok. In November 1942, she traveled to Grodno to try to help the Jews in the two ghettos there when they came under Gestapo rule. She continued her efforts until February 1943 when the last Jews were removed, then returned to Bialystok to warn the ghetto inhabitants there that they, too, would be liquidated. Her unit managed to get a few members of the resistance into a nearby forest. She participated in the Bialystok uprising in August 1943 and was forced to retreat until she hit barbed wire. She then survived strafing from a German plane and managed to elude the SS infantry until she found herself surrounded by a group about to be transported. She managed to sneak outside a little-used gate into the factory area, then, using an old pass she found in her pocket, got past the Germans into the forest to a camp of about fifty Resistance fighters. She returned to Bialystok and continued her work until the liberation.

After the liberation, Grossman served as Ha-Shomer ha-Tsa'ir representative in institutions set up by surviving Jews in Poland. In 1948 she moved to Israel and joined the Kibbutz Evron in western Galilee where she remained politically active. She was a member of the Knesset (Israeli parliament) from 1969 to 1981 and again beginning in 1984. She wrote her experiences in *People of the Underground* in 1965 and published an English language version entitled *The Underground Army: Fighters of the Bialystok Ghetto* in 1987.

## BIBLIOGRAPHY

Grossman, Haika. *The Underground Army: Fighters of the Bialystok Ghetto*. New York: Holocaust Library, 1987; Syrkin, M. *Blessed is the Match*. Philadelphia, Pa.: Transcontinental, 1976; EncHol.

# H

## HARNACK, MILDRED FISH

(1902–1943)
**Political Prisoner, United States**

Mildred Fish Harnack, the only known American woman tried by a Nazi military tribunal and hanged on express orders of Adolf Hitler, was born in Milwaukee, Wisconsin, on September 16, 1902. She attended George Washington University and received a Ph.D. from the University of Wisconsin at Madison. While at the University of Wisconsin she met Arvid Harnack, a German economics student on a Rockefeller scholarship, and the two were married.

In the early 1930s, the People's University of Berlin invited Mildred Harnack to conduct a series of lectures on American literature. In 1938, the young couple returned to America for an extended visit. Upon their return to Germany, her husband became involved in anti-Nazi politics and was committed to the goals of the Red Orchestra, a Resistance group. Although Mildred's mother begged her to return to America, she refused to be separated from her husband. Although she was Jewish, Mildred felt she was safe in Germany and that her U.S. citizenship would protect her.

In September 1942, the Gestapo arrested the couple, and four months later, on December 15, 1942, they were brought to trial with eleven others, including three other women. All except Mildred were German or

Austrian citizens. They were accused of involvement in the Red Orchestra and one week later all but two were found guilty of treason and executed the next day. Mildred and Countess Erika von Brock Dorff received sentences of six and ten years, respectively. In Mildred's case, the Germans failed to prove that she knew of her husband's involvement or whether she had participated in the Red Orchestra. As was the custom, her sentence was forwarded to Adolf Hitler for confirmation. Reports suggest that he was furious at the light sentences given the women and ordered them tried again. They were condemned to death in January 1943. The execution was delayed several times because of "unusual circumstances" and the fact that Harnack was an American citizen. Harnack spent the time translating verses of Goethe and, according to the prison chaplain, carried on "passionate dialogues" with a portrait of her mother. He noted that she neither smiled nor wept.

Family and friends tried to save her, but Arvid's cousin, Axel von Harnack, was warned against "any approaches in favor of this woman"; he was told to act as if she had "nothing to do with you" (Davies, 379). Her execution was set for February 16 and, according to Nazi law, would be carried out by decapitation. Hitler insisted, however, that Harnack be executed by slow strangulation as the men had been, saying the indignity "befitted the foreign wife of a traitor" (Davies, 379).

In 1961 an American lawyer, Peter Davies, attempted to obtain recognition for Harnack, but the State Department denied the request. Assistant Secretary of State Brook Hays explained that Harnack had not been associated with the U.S. government and that it was not usual for the government to recognize this type of "covert action." Despite the fact that she had not been involved in the Red Orchestra, the government had only the Nazi trial to go by.

**BIBLIOGRAPHY**

Davies, Peter. "No Nameless Heroes." *Christian Century*, April 16, 1975, 377–81; Stiles, Kent B. *Postal Saints and Sinners*. New York: Theodore Gans' Sons, 1964; Kohn, Kathe, and Reinhold Schneider. *Dying We Live*. New York: Pantheon, 1956; BioIn 10; InWom.

# HAUTVAL, ADELAIDE

**(1906–   )**
**Physician, Camp Prisoner, Lithuania**

Adelaide Hautval, who, along with Dorota Kleinova and Alina Brewda, practiced medicine at Auschwitz concentration camp, was born in 1906.

Adelaide Hautval. Yad Vashem Photo Archives, courtesy of USHMM Photo Archives.

She received her medical education in Strasbourg, France, and practiced in psychiatric clinics there and in Switzerland. In April 1942, she attempted to cross the border between the occupied and the unoccupied zones in France to attend her mother's funeral and was arrested for not having a permit. Officials took her to Bourges prison where she was very outspoken about the treatment of Jewish prisoners. She was transferred to Romainville prison and finally to Auschwitz in January 1943.

In addition to her regular duties at Auschwitz, she helped hide women suffering from typhus on the top floor of her block and treated them as well as possible without medicine or supplies. When the garrison doctor, Eduard Wirths, asked her to practice gynecology, she accepted. Like Brewda and Kleinova, she knew the Nazis were conducting experiments in sterilization in Block 10 and she wanted to learn more about them. She discovered that a team of three doctors, Horst Schumann, Wladyslaw Dering, and Carl Clauberg, was sterilizing women by overdosing them with X rays and performing ovariectomies (removal of the ovaries). They were conducting the experiments in order to eventually sterilize all Jews, both male and female. Once Hautval discovered the nature of the experiments, she vehemently refused to participate. Amazingly, camp officials did not punish her for her refusal but allowed her to continue practicing medicine at Birkenau (Auschwitz II) until she was transferred to Ravensbruck in August 1944. The camp was liberated in April 1945.

Like Brewda, Hautval was called as a witness in a libel trial initiated by Wladyslaw Dering against Leon Uris, the author. Dering sued Uris for slander in his book *Exodus*. The prosecution used Hautval to refute Dering's claim that he could not refuse to carry out the experiments since she had done so and had not been punished. The judge, Justice Frederick Horace Lawton, called her "one of the most impressive and courageous women who have [*sic*] ever given evidence in the courts of this country." The following year she was named a "Righteous Among Nations" by Yad Vashem.

### BIBLIOGRAPHY

Hill, Mavis, and L. Norman Williams. *Auschwitz in England: A Record of a Libel Action*. New York: Ballantine Books, 1965; EncHol.

## HIGGINS, MARGUERITE

**(1920–1966)**
**War Correspondent, United States**

Marguerite Higgins, one of the first war correspondents to enter the concentration camps of Dachau and Buchenwald after their liberation, was born on September 3, 1920, in Hong Kong to Lawrence and Marguerite Goddard Higgins. She received a B.A. cum laude from the University of California and an M.S. from Columbia University. In 1942 she was the second woman hired as a straight news reporter on the *New York Herald Tribune* after obtaining an interview with the elusive Madame Chiang

Marguerite Higgins. Courtesy of the National Archives.

Kai-shek. She quickly became one of the *Tribune's* star reporters and aggressively campaigned for an overseas assignment. She won her assignment and with seven other war correspondents sailed on the converted troop ship *Queen Mary.*

Higgins arrived in London in 1944, where she waited anxiously for orders to Europe before the war ended. She was devastated when she contracted jaundice and was hospitalized, but by February 1945 she was ready to join the other correspondents in France. She attended daily press conferences given by Gen. Dwight D. Eisenhower and covered the trial of Admiral Jean Pierre Esteva for high treason. In March she received word that she would be traveling with the Eighth Army Air Force and a half-dozen other journalists to look at heavily bombed German areas. Carrying a typewriter, sleeping bag, and a few extra clothes, the twenty-five-year-old Higgins joined the Seventh Army on the road to Munich. She toured the city of Frankfurt then hitched a ride on a cargo plane carrying barrels of gasoline to Gen. George S. Patton's Third Army tank division. After landing at the Weimar air strip, she persuaded a Third Army jeep driver to take her to Buchenwald. She entered the concentration camp only hours after Patton had liberated it. She interrogated inmates and collected names of victims and guards and the dates and details of mass executions. She interviewed survivors who had seen guards force the victims into the gas chambers, and she accompanied a group of Germans ordered to view Buchenwald as a lesson in man's inhumanity to man.

After covering Buchenwald, Higgins and another correspondent, Peter Furst, set off across German territory, accepting the surrender of various Germans along the way and piling their jeep high with surrendered weapons.

In April 1945, Higgins filed the story of the secret correspondence of Dr. Alfred Rosenberg, the chief political philosopher and formulator of the Nazi racial theory. She and Furst had discovered his papers in a subterranean cellar five stories below the sixteenth-century Lichtenfels Castle. After that, Furst and Higgins rushed on, hoping to be the first reporters to reach Dachau. When they arrived, two American divisions were still fighting the Germans on the northern outskirts of the concentration camp. They detoured around the fighting, headed for the administration buildings that supposedly had been liberated, and came upon boxcars filling with rotting corpses. Two jeeps of the Forty-second Infantry arrived and Higgins and Furst followed them inside the camp, where an SS general was holding a large white flag. They accepted the surrender of twenty-two guards and ordered them to open the gate to the camp. The prisoners came streaming from the barracks and the two correspondents found themselves being hugged and kissed by hundreds of men after Higgins announced in English, German, and French that they were free. Higgins received the army campaign ribbon for outstanding service with the armed forces under difficult conditions for her participation that day and was named best foreign correspondent by the New York Newspaper Women's Club. After the war the paper assigned Higgins to cover the war crimes trials at Nuremberg.

Higgins continued her career as a correspondent until 1966. In 1950 she was named chief of the Far East bureau. She covered the Korean War and made headlines herself when she and other American women correspondents were ordered to leave Korea by Lt. Gen. Walton H. Walker. Higgins contacted General of the Army Douglas MacArthur and he rescinded the order the next day. She and a fellow *Herald Tribune* reporter, Homer Bigart, shared the Pulitzer Prize for the best coverage of the Korean War in 1951. She also published her first book, *War in Korea*, in 1951, followed by *News Is a Singular Thing* (1956) and *Tales of the Foreign Service* (1963). She died on January 3, 1966, of leishmaniasis, a disease caused by the bite of a sand fly that she contracted on a tour of Vietnam, India and Pakistan.

**BIBLIOGRAPHY**

Obituary in *New York Herald Tribune*, January 4, 1966; obituary in NewYT, January 4, 1966; 27; obituary in *Time*, January 14, 1966; May, Antoinette. *Witness to War: A Biography of Marguerite Higgins*. New York: Beaufort Books, 1983; CurBio 51, 66; WhoAmJ 58, 64, 66; AnnObit of 79; WhAm 4; AmWomWr; BioIn 2, 3, 4, 5, 6, 7, 8, 9, 12; ConAu5R; ConAu25R; InWom; NotAW: Mod.

# HOHENLOHE-WALDENBURG, STEFANIE RICHTER

**(1896– )**
**Deportee, Austria**

Stefanie Hohenlohe-Waldenburg, called "the mystery woman of Europe," was said to have been born into a middle-class Jewish family named Richter in Vienna in 1896. On May 12, 1914, she married Prince Friedrich Franz Hohenlohe-Waldenburg, but they were divorced in 1920. In 1931 it was rumored that she arranged a massive loan for Adolf Hitler through pro-German publisher Lord Rothermere. She was introduced to Josef Goebbels, Hitler's minister of propaganda, who attempted to recruit her into the Nazi Party. They gave her the title "Honorary Aryan."

In 1933 the French Press reported that she had been expelled from France for being a Nazi spy. She received a letter from German Consul General Weidemann who said Hitler would grant her any help he could to "reestablish her personal honor and financial status." In 1938 she played hostess during Viscount Runciman's visit to Prague and arranged meetings that later resulted in the Munich Pact. In 1939 she sued Lord Rothermere in London for services as a "foreign political representative." The dispute involved monies paid—she said that he paid her $185,000; he said that he paid her $250,000. The judge ruled against Hohenlohe-Waldenburg saying he was satisfied Lord Rothermere never promised contractually to give her £5,000 a year for life.

On December 23, 1939, Hohenlohe-Waldenburg arrived in New York with her son and mother. The U.S. government denied her request for renewal of her temporary visitor's permit, and she was told to leave the United States by December 21, 1940, or deportation proceedings would be initiated. She was linked to Captain Fritz Weidemann, German Consul at San Francisco, and described as "inimical" to America's best interests because of her "close association with the Nazis" (CurBio, 1940, 395). Little has been heard of her since.

**BIBLIOGRAPHY**

E. M. "Persons and Personages: The Nazi Princess." LIV AGE, March 1939, 43–46; *New York Post*, January 12, 1940, 1; NewYT, November 16, 1939, 25; NewYT, December 8, 1939, 5; *Time*, November 20, 1939, 24+; CurBio, 1940, 395–96; InWom.

# HUCH, RICARDA OCTAVIA

**(1864–1947)**
**Author, Resistance Worker, Germany**

Ricarda Octavia Huch was born in Brunswick (Braunschweig), Germany, on August 18, 1864. Huch was the first woman admitted to the University of Zurich and obtained a Ph.D. in 1892. From 1892 to 1896 she was secretary of the city library of Zurich. In 1897 she moved to Vienna to write after her marriage to Dr. Ermanno Ceconi, a dentist. The two divorced in 1906, and in 1917 she married a cousin, Richard Huch. In 1924 she became an honorary senator of the University of Munich. Three years later she was honored at the Prussian Academy of the Arts for her writing, which consisted mainly of romantic and historical novels and historical monographs. In 1931 officials awarded her the Goethe Prize of the city of Frankfurt for her writing. She resigned from the Academy of Prussian Writers in 1933 to protest the expulsion by the Nazis of writers such as Heinrich Mann and Alfred Doblin and began writing letters to the president of the Akadamie der Kunste about the menace of National Socialism.

In 1934 Huch was elected to the Nazi Academy of Writers but declined to become a member. She was described as close to the Lutheran opposition to the Nazis and the anti-Hitler conspirators of July 20, 1944. It was later speculated that she was secretly collecting material for a book on the anti-Nazi underground movement while working on a three-volume history of Germany, *Deutsche Geschichte* (1934, 1937, 1949). Her opposition to the Nazi view of history prevented publication of the last volume until after World War II. Although she and her family had trouble with the Nazi authorities, they managed to escape imprisonment. She died in 1947 while writing a collection of biographies of German Resistance fighters. The book was completed after her death by Gunther Welsenborn (*Der lautlose Aufstand* or *The Silent Rebellion*, 1953).

## BIBLIOGRAPHY

Heller, Otto. *Studies in Modern German Literature*. New York: Gin, 1905; Edinger, D. "Ricarda Huch," *Nation*, May 1, 1948, 466; obituary in NewYT, November 20, 1947, 30; *Wilson Library Bulletin* 22 (January 1948): 354; AnnObit of 79; WhE&EA; EncTR; EncWL 2; InWom; IntDcWB; BioIn 1, 2, 3, 4; ModGL; OxGer; REn; TwCA; TwCA Supp.

# J

## JONGH, ANDRÉE DE

**(1916–   )**
**Resistance Fighter, Belgium**

Andrée de Jongh was living at home in the Schaerbeek district of Brussels with her father, Frederic de Jongh, a schoolmaster, when World War II began. She was interested in art, but trained to become a nurse and was working in a Belgian hospital for wounded British soldiers in 1940. With help from her family, de Jongh helped set up the Comet Line, an escape route for more than 800 Allied airmen and soldiers from Brussels by way of Paris to Bilbao and Gibraltar.

In 1941 de Jongh fled to Bilbao across the Pyrénées on foot and approached the British Consulate about working for their agencies. She was given the code name "Postman" and established the line between Brussels and St. Jean-de-Luz as an escape route. She organized couriers to carry messages along the line, including messages to her father. Between July and October 1942, de Jongh and her Basque guide, Florentino Gioechea, led fifty-four men over the Pyrénées. Meanwhile, the Gestapo was still trying to find her and placed a price on her father's head of 1 million Belgian francs.

In January 1942, de Jongh paid a secret visit to her father in Brussels and barely escaped through the backyard before two officers of the Secret Field Police arrived at the house. On April 30, 1942 her father left for

Paris. She and her father continued to help British airmen to escape from France to Spain. Her sister Suzanne was arrested and sent first to the Mauthausen concentration camp and then to Ravensbruck. In the spring of 1943 Andrée de Jongh was arrested on the Spanish frontier and taken to Fresnes prison, then Ravensbruck. Officials eventually transferred her to Germany, but the Germans did not realize her involvement in the Comet Line, so of twenty-three people scheduled to be executed, she alone survived. She was liberated and after the war worked with lepers in Addis Ababa and Senegal. She received the George Medal, the highest award civilians can earn in Great Britain.

### BIBLIOGRAPHY

Heave, Airey. "Postman Across the Pyrenees." In *Women in the Resistance and in the Holocaust: The Voices of Eyewitnesses*, edited by Vera Laska, (129–36). Westport, Conn.: Greenwood Press, 1983; WhoWWII.

# K

## KASPRZAK, IDA DOBRZANSKA

**(1923–  )**
**Resistance Fighter, Poland**

Ida Kasprzak, one of 40,000 women members of the Home Army in Poland, was born January 17, 1923. In 1941 she joined the underground in Warsaw and then, along with her widowed mother, older sister, and younger brother, joined the Home Army. Kasprzak worked in an office and at lunchtime, after work, and on weekends she smuggled guns. On January 17, 1944, she received a revolver in a Je Reviens perfume box for her birthday. She got to use it when she and other women were traveling underground to a meeting and two drunken Poles carrying bloody sticks accosted them. Kasprzak held them off with the gun and locked them in a nearby building. Her commander later tried to confiscate her gun, but she refused to give it up.

Kasprzak was made an officer in the Home Army in charge of a group of thirty female medics who carried the wounded to safety and applied first aid, often while under fire. In one of these instances, Kasprzak was carrying a 200-pound man to safety when a piece of shrapnel headed for her stomach but fell before it reached her body. She picked it up and carried it through the war as a reminder of the work she needed to do.

Once the wounded were picked up, the women delivered them to a hospital set up in a former shoe store. The chief surgeon was a veterinarian, and anesthesia consisted of liquor cordial. Hospital aides were prostitutes from nearby areas. The hospital was eventually overflowing when the city was in flames and the fighting was "floor by floor" in the surrounding buildings. At one point, the women came upon two bodies that had been lying in the streets for a week. Kasprzak volunteered to find three other women to retrieve the bodies. Wearing white overcoats with red crosses on the arms, sides, and backs, they made their way to the German commander across the street and asked to retrieve the bodies. He agreed and gave the command to hold fire. They dug graves and buried the bodies. Afterwards, two German soldiers used the women as human shields to make their way two miles through the city.

By September 4, 1944, Kasprzak's unit was without food and medical supplies. When an eighty-year-old woman offered Kasprzak a chicken leg, she cried. Her brother had been killed and her mother and sister, fighting in another part of the city, had been captured and sent to Ravensbruck. On October 5 Kasprzak was captured and sent to Bergen-Belsen, south of Hamburg, Germany, where she was placed with 4,000 Polish women and became commanding officer of her barracks. She met Black Barbara (Irena Komorowski), a fellow resistance fighter, for the first time. In April 1945, Gen. George S. Patton liberated the camp and Kasprzak was sent to England and then posted to Germany. She eventually immigrated to Toronto. She suffered physically and psychologically from the effects of the war. For instance, at the age of twenty-seven she was said to have had the stomach of a ninety-year-old woman.

**BIBLIOGRAPHY**

Saywell, Shelley. "Uprising: Poland, 1939–45." In *Women in War* (102–129). New York: Viking Penguin Inc., 1985.

## KATONA, EDITA

(1913–   )
**French Spy, Austria**

Edita Katona was born on August 10, 1913, in Vienna, Austria, to Hugo and Anna Pernitzova Zuckermann. She studied in Austria and Switzerland before the family was exiled in Monte Carlo in 1938. From 1938 to 1944, Katona was a member of the Deuxième Bureau (the French Espionage department), involved in intelligence work. She was paid 3,000 francs a month and held the rank of sub-lieutenant in the French Navy. Her first assignment was to report on shipping and photograph airfield defenses in Palermo, Italy. When she returned to Monte Carlo, Deuxième authorities found she had accidentally stolen a map marked with all the defense areas in Sicily.

Katona made a second trip to Palermo to photograph coastal defenses. Her mother accompanied her on this assignment as well as on many others. Her third trip to Italy involved finding out when construction of the battleships *Duilio* and *Giulio Cesare* would be completed; Deuxième authorities speculated Italy would not go to war until the ships were completed. Although the location of the two ships was unknown, Katona found the ships in Genoa and successfully photographed them. Her superiors then sent Katona and her mother to Venice, where Edita set up an espionage network and photographed the island naval base of Marghera. Additionally, in 1942 she arranged to have the head of the Italian secret police, Giuseppe Castellano, defect by offering him three million francs for the Italian Naval Code.

In July 1940 the Bureau lent her to the Troisième Bureau, the counter-espionage department of French Intelligence, where she worked under the code name of "Marianne Chabot." In the summer of 1942 they sent Katona to photograph the Straits of Messina. Back in Paris, when the Germans demanded that all Jews holding German passports be handed over to French authorities, she and her mother began hiding Jews. (At one time they had twenty-two people hiding in their apartment.) They returned to Italy in 1942 and in October, while Edita was on assignment, her mother was arrested and put in a prison run by nuns in Genoa; there she committed suicide in November to insure she did not betray her daughter under torture.

By November 1942, Katona was the second most-wanted person in Nice because of her spying activities—the first was another agent, Simon Cotoni—and she went into hiding. The Bureau spirited her out of the city by train in the company of Pierre Sauvaire, Commissaire de Police. She made her way to Paris and began visiting a canteen for German soldiers where she learned secrets and passed them along to the agency. She was interrogated by the Gestapo and released and, ironically, picked up by Resistance fighters because they thought she was a German spy. They held her in Fresnes prison until one of the younger fighters contacted police who verified her identity. In 1944 she received the Croix de Combatant, and in 1945 she received the Croix de Guerre.

BIBLIOGRAPHY

Katona, Edita, with Patrick Magnaghten. *Code-Name Marianne*. New York: David McKay Company, 1976; BioIn II; ConAu 69.

# KEUN, IRMGARD

(1905–1982)
Author, Germany

Irmgard Keun, whose writing was banned in Nazi Germany, was born in Berlin, Germany, in 1905. In 1913 the family moved to Cologne, where her father was director of an oil refinery. She attended the girls' lyceum, then went to work for her father. In 1923 she attended acting school in Cologne but returned to office work three years later. She began writing novels and became famous overnight. When the Nazis came to power, they targeted her books because of her criticism of their defamation of German womanhood, liberal sexual mores, and irreverence for traditional values. In the spring of 1933 they put her name on an official blacklist for the "purification" of bookstores, and her books were confiscated and destroyed. Newspapers were no longer allowed to publish her short pieces.

On September 22, 1933, the Reich Chamber Law was passed, instructing that anyone involved in producing culture had to belong to one of seven departments. Keun was refused admittance to the Reich Chamber of Literature, despite repeated attempts. On October 29, 1935, she sued the government, trying to reclaim the income lost because of the confiscation of her books. It was rumored that the Gestapo arrested and tortured her, and she was freed only after her father paid a large ransom. Whatever the reason, on May 4, 1936, she was forced to emigrate to the Netherlands so she could continue her writing.

From 1936 to 1938 she published four books and visited the United States on a small stipend from the American Guild for Cultural Freedom. She returned to the Netherlands and two years later the Nazis swept through the Low Countries and occupied the Netherlands. She went underground and returned to her family in Cologne using false papers and a fake press release that said she had committed suicide. Back in Germany she made no secret of her opposition to the Nazis. Her brother Gerd was killed in Russia, and bombs and artillery raids destroyed the family's homes. After the war Keun lived with little food, furniture, or clothing in her parents' bombed-out house in Cologne. She began writing again then dropped out of sight. In the mid-1970s, she was rediscovered living in poverty in an attic room in Bonn. She had spent four-and-a-half months in the state hospital in Duren in 1962 for alcoholism, and six years in a Bonn hospital; she was released in 1972. There was a resurgence of interest in her work and she read from her novels, gave interviews, and had her books republished. She died on May 5, 1982, of a lung tumor.

## BIBLIOGRAPHY

Horsley, Ritta Jo. "Irmgard Keun." In *Women Writers of Austria, Germany and Switzerland: An Annotated Bio-Bibliographical Guide*, edited by Elke Frederiksen. Westport, Conn.: Greenwood Publishing, 1970; Lensing, Leo. "Cinema, Society, and Literature in Irmgard Keun's 'Das kunsteidene Madchen.' " *Germanic Review* 60 (Fall 1985): 129–34; DcLB 69.

# KLEIST, RUTH VON

(1867–1945)
**Resistance Fighter, Prussia**

Ruth von Kleist was born on February 4, 1867, to Robert and Agnes von Rohr, Count and Countess of Zedlitz and Trutzschler in Grossenboran, Prussia. She was convent-schooled and in 1886 married Jurgen von Kleist. Von Kleist died in 1896, leaving her with five children. She organized her properties into one of the most productive in the district's history during World War I and lost a son in 1917 when his plane crashed. In 1925 Ruth von Kleist became aware of the radical views of Elisabeth von Thadden and wrote *The Responsibility of Landed Property in This Social Crisis* (1925), which discussed feudal institutions in democratic nation-states.

In 1931 von Kleist's granddaughter, Raba Roberta Stahlberg, became the first woman in the family to attend a university where she joined the Nazi party and became the leader of the female Studer faction under Dr. Josef Goebbels, Nazi minister of propaganda. The rest of the family, however, was totally opposed to Nazism. When it was found the family contained one-fourth Jewish blood, Nazi officials purged her father from the Provincial Registry. On April 1, 1933, the day of a national boycott of Jewish-owned businesses, von Kleist invited a Jewish business-owner to tea.

In 1935 von Kleist became a delegate to the Belgrade District governing board of the Confessing Church that consisted of Protestant clergymen, lay people, and members of the congregation who refused to participate in the new German Christian Church. She began providing food, furniture, kitchen and writing utensils, books, and gardening tools for the persecuted. Von Kleist helped raise money for the Bonhoeffer seminary at Finkenwalde. She formed a study club in her home and read and discussed Bonhoeffer's published tracts. Church officials gave her the task of praying for every person on a list of seminarians and pastors who were Jewish by birth or had Jewish wives, eventually about 804 in number, and she was in charge of working with the relatives of those imprisoned in Finkenwalde. Her home became a haven for the Bonhoeffers and two rooms in her house became guest rooms for Jews. When Bonhoeffer's church closed, she and her grandchildren attended churches whose pastors resisted Nazism. She was also at work writing a book, *Why Should One Read The Bible.*

In 1939 the German government called up Bonhoeffer for military service, and von Kleist intervened to get him released. She was unable to help her son, six grandsons, and son-in-law the next year when they were called into the military. When the Nazis prevented Bonhoeffer from preaching and were monitoring his activities, he took up residence with von Kleist. In January 1941, the seventy-four-year-old von Kleist had a stroke and one of her six grandsons, Hans Friedrich, was killed in battle. The next year her son-in-law also died in battle. On March 2, 1945, as the Russians advanced on the countryside, von Kleist was placed on a wagon and forced to seek cover in the forest for six days and nights as thousands of tanks and soldiers passed by. When she returned to the road, she was stopped and ordered to return home without food or horses. Russian soldiers placed her in a peasant's hut where she lived for two weeks. In April 1945, von Kleist returned to her home to find the Russians had stripped it of its furnishings, including the bathtub and toilet, and were using it as a dairy. During the trip she had lost her wedding rings and glasses and by now was lame and nearly blind. Despite her misfortunes, she began teaching kindergarten and Bible classes to her great grandchildren in a nearby schoolhouse. On September 8, 1945, she fell and broke a leg. There was no plaster to set her leg and she contracted pneumonia while recuperating. She died on October 1, 1945, and was buried between her husband, Jurgen, and son, Konstantin.

BIBLIOGRAPHY

Pejsa, Jane. *Matriarch of Conspiracy: Ruth von Kleist, 1867–1945*. Minneapolis, Minn.: Kenwood Publishing, 1991.

# KLUGER, RUTH

**(1916–1980)**
**Rescuer, USSR**

Called "Lady Israel," Ruth Kluger was the only female member of Mossad, one of the largest secret rescue movements for getting Jews out of Nazi-occupied Europe. She was born Ruth Polisiuk in Kiev, Russia, in 1916, but grew up in the Rumanian town of Czernowitz where she eventually learned to speak eight languages. She obtained a law degree from the University of Vienna. She married Emmanuel Kluger in 1934 and emigrated to Palestine. She was an office worker in Tel Aviv when Berl Katznelson, editor of *Darvar*, a Jewish newspaper, and Elishu Columb, commander in chief of the underground Jewish Army, the Haganah, recruited her. She joined the Mossad, the organization that led the Jewish underground rescue movement, and returned to Rumania where she worked on getting Jews out of Hitler's Europe.

One of Kluger's biggest efforts came in November 1939, when the *Hilda* was set to sail for Palestine with more than 700 Jews on board. She received a cable saying the ship was frozen to the pier in Balchik, on the coast of the Black Sea in Bulgaria. The ship had been waiting for more refugees to arrive aboard a cruise ship moving down the Danube to the Black Sea, but the cruise ship was frozen as well. The sailors in Balchik had mutinied and were running amok through the town. Town authorities were demanding that the ship leave as soon as the ice broke, and the 727 passengers were threatening to tell the world of the living conditions on board the ship. Kluger set off for Balchik across the snow. On arriving there, she arranged to take empty sleighs to a nearby town to get food to replace the depleted supplies in Balchik. Then she hired men to carry barrels of water to an abandoned Turkish bath high above the city so that the refugees could have their first bath in weeks. She met with the passengers under cover of darkness to protect her identity and gave a stirring speech urging them to persevere. After a fire on board and a storm that drove the ship out to sea, Kluger decided to let it sail without the additional refugees who had not arrived and the 727 refugees on board the *Hilda* arrived safely in Palestine.

In another instance, the refugee ship *Tiger Hill* was discovered and seized by the Rumanian government. Kluger arranged its release and the ship sailed to Tel Aviv and discharged its 834 passengers in shallow water off the beach. The refugees changed into beach clothes and disappeared into the crowd of sunbathers.

In December 1940, Iron Guardists (a Romanian anti-semitic group) arrived to arrest Kluger, but she escaped out a bathroom window and made her way to Turkey. Meanwhile, her brother David, his wife Sophie, and their two children were in forced labor camps, and her brother Arthur was in an Austrian concentration camp. After obtaining 250 legal certificates for children to go to Palestine on April 6, 1941, Kluger's superiors sent her to Egypt to raise money and organize a rescue mission to bring Jews from Egypt, Lebanon, and Syria into Palestine.

In 1945 she was sent to Europe as an official representative of the Jews of Palestine. She was the first Jew of Palestine to enter one of the death camps a day or so after Allied troops opened them.

In 1946 Kluger helped bring 3,000 refugee children from southern France to Palestine on the ship *Ascania*. When the state of Israel was created in 1948, she was given the Hebrew surname of Aliau and eventually worked in public relations for the Zim Navigating Company. She chaired the Public Relations Association in Tel Aviv and was on the executive board of the International Public Relations Association. She died in February 1980.

**BIBLIOGRAPHY**

Kluger, Ruth, and Peggy Mann. *The Secret Ship*. Garden City, N.Y.: Doubleday, 1978; Kluger, Ruth, and Peggy Mann. *The Launching of the Largest Secret Rescue Movement of All Times*. Garden City, N.Y.: Doubleday, 1973; BioIn 10; ConAu 108; AnnObit of 80.

# KOLLWITZ, KATHE

(1867–1945)
**Artist, Germany**

Kathe Kollwitz, a German artist, was born in the East Prussian town of Konigsberg. Her father and grandfather were both preachers in the Free Congregation Church and she grew up in a liberal, intellectual environment. Her father, Karl Schmidt, encouraged her to become an artist and she began studying with a local engraver. She attended the Art School for Girls in Berlin and when she became engaged, her father sent her to the Women's Art School in Munich for two years to insure that she continued her education rather than get married. She eventually did marry her fiancé, Karl Kollwitz, at age twenty-three, but continued her career. Her graphic series, The Weavers, depicting Berlin's poverty-stricken workers, was shown in the Berlin Art Exhibition of 1898. The jury awarded her a gold medal, but the Kaiser vetoed it because The Weavers showed Germany in a negative light. She won a gold medal the next year at Dresden and was invited to teach graphic arts and life drawing at the Art School for Girls in Berlin.

When she was in her thirties, Kollwitz began studying sculpture in Paris, and in 1907 she won the prestigious Villa Romana Prize and spent a year in Florence. In October 1914, her son Peter was killed on the battlefield of Flanders. Kollwitz created life-size granite figures she called Father and Mother Mourning. Other subjects of war followed into the 1940s, and when she depicted mothers standing in a circle defending their children, the Nazis forbade their display saying, "in the Third Reich mothers have no need to defend their children. The State does that" (Nagel, 6). The Nazis also removed her pieces that had been displayed in the Crown Prince Palace in Berlin to the cellar. She was forced to resign her professorship at the Prussian Academy of Art and give up her spacious studio. She was expelled from all official positions, forbidden to exhibit her work, and finally forbidden to work at all. Her husband died in 1940, and when Berlin was bombed, the Allies evacuated her to the countryside; her home of fifty years was destroyed. She died in 1945 at seventy-seven years old, a few days before the end of the war.

## BIBLIOGRAPHY

Kollwitz, Kathe (Schmidt). *Diary and Letters*. Edited by Hans Kollwitz. London: Regency, 1955; Canada, J. "Tragic World of Kathe Kollwitz." *New York Times Magazine*, November 5, 1966, 44–45; Klein, Mina C., and H. Arthur Klein. *Kathe Kollwitz: Life in Art*. New York: Holt, 1972; Nagel, Otto. *Kathe Kollwitz*. Trans. Stella Humphries. New York: New York Graphic Society, 1971; Moffat, Mary Jane, and C. Painter, eds. "Kathe Kollwitz (1867–1945)." In *Revelations: Diaries of Women* (237–52). New York: Random House, 1974; Munsterberg, Hugo. *History of Women Artists*. New York: Potter, 1975, 111–15; Harris, Ann Sutherland, and Linda Hochlin. *Women Artists: 1550–1950*. New York: Knopf, 1976, 263–65; Kearns, Martha. *Kathe Kollwitz: Woman and Artist*. New York: Feminist Press, 1976; Hinz, Renate. *Kathe Kollwitz: Graphics, Posters, Drawings*. Trans. Rita Kimber and Robert Kimber. New York: Pantheon Books, 1981; Prelinger, Elizabeth. *Kathe

*Kollwitz.* Washington, D.C.: National Gallery of Art, 1992; Kollwitz, Kathe. "Kathe Kollwitz: A Self Portrait." *New York Times Magazine*, October 17, 1948, 24+; BioIn 1, 2, 4, 6, 8, 9, 10, 11, 12; EncTR; GoodHS; HerW; IntDcWB; WhoWNG; OxGer; TwCA; WomA; WhAm 4.

# KOLMAR, GERTRUD

**(1894–1943)**
**Poet, Germany**

Gertrud Kolmar, one of the most important female poets in Germany, was born in December 1894 in a Berlin suburb. She became fluent in French, English, and Russian and worked as a translator and interpreter in the German Foreign Office. She also worked as a postal censor and with prisoners of war during World War I. After World War I she became a teacher and private tutor, specializing in working with children who were deaf and unable to speak. In 1917 she published her first book of forty poems, *Gedichte*. The 1930s saw the death of her mother. After her younger sister escaped to Switzerland, Kolmar remained behind in Germany to care for her aging father. Although Kolmar had an unhappy love affair and never married, two of her poems that praised love, female sexuality, motherhood, and children appeared in the prestigious *Insel Almanac*.

In 1938 Kolmar published a book of poems entitled *The Woman and the Beast*, possibly the last book published by Jewish publishers in Germany. She was hailed as a poet with extraordinary talent. In February 1938 she wrote her last letter to her sister in Switzerland while she was working as a slave laborer pasting cartons in a munitions factory. The Nazis had sent her eighty-year-old father to Theresienstadt and eventually Kolmar, too, perished in a concentration camp, possibly Auschwitz sometime between February 1943 and the end of the war in 1947. Jacob Picard in *Commentary* magazine called her the greatest lyrical Jewish poet who ever lived (460).

**BIBLIOGRAPHY**

Langer, L. L. "Survival Through Art: The Career of Gertrud Kolmar." *Leo Baeck Institute Yearbook* 23. London: Secker and Warburg, 1978, 247–58; Picard, Jacob. "Gertrud Kolmar: The Woman and the Beasts." *Commentary*, November 1950, 459–65; Hamburger, M. "German-Jewish Poetess." *Commentary*, January 1957, 99–100; BioIn 2, 4, 11; EncWL; EncWL 2; ModGL; OxGer.

# KOMOROWSKI, IRENA KWIATKOWSKA

(?–?)
**Resistance Fighter, Poland**

Irena Komorowski was a young medical student at the University of Warsaw and was among the first to join the Polish underground in 1941. She joined the Home Army and was given the code name "Barbara" from a popular children's story. Unfortunately, others had the same idea so she became known as "Black Barbara" because of her black hair. By 1942 she was helping with organizational work and carried messages from unit to unit throughout the city. She planned strategies to take over small towns and railway stations. She obtained information booklets about German arms shipments that allowed simpler versions of guns to be manufactured. She communicated information to England and kept track of passwords and routes as they became unsafe to use.

On August 1, 1944, Soviet troops invaded Poland and a trip to work that usually took forty-five minutes took from six o'clock in the morning until two o'clock in the afternoon. Komorowski continued her work as a courier despite the fact that shootouts in the streets were common and that the German Luftwaffe was dropping bombs. She often planned her route through bombed-out buildings because they were less likely targets. Once, when she was cornered by snipers and she had to crawl to safety, the gold medallion she wore around her neck saved her life when a bullet hit it. On August 29 Home Army officials gave Komorowski the order to leave using the sewers. She and others held onto a string as they made their way through knee-high waste matter. They stopped at every manhole to listen for Germans, fearful that the Nazis might throw a grenade down. They emerged nine hours later.

By September 4 Komorowski was working in a shoe store that the Home Army had turned into a hospital. Medical supplies, food, lights, and water were severely limited. On October 2 the hospital staff surrendered to the Germans and she joined about 1,000 other female prisoners going to Germany. Komorowski was sent to Bergen-Belsen, south of Hamburg, where she met Ida Dobrzanska Kasprzak, who had also been in the Home Army. Komorowski was sent to England after Gen. George S. Patton liberated the camp in April 1945. She continued to serve as an officer and was posted to Germany. During the years after the war, Komorowski, like many other women, suffered from post-traumatic stress syndrome. She married a Polish soldier and moved to

Canada where she worked in the trauma room at Toronto General Hospital.

**BIBLIOGRAPHY**

Saywell, Shelley. "Uprising: Poland, 1939–45." *Women in War* (102–130). New York: Viking Penguin, Inc., 1985.

## KORCZAK-MARLA, ROZKA

(?–1988)
**Zionist, Resistance Fighter, Poland**

Rozka Korczak-Marla was born in Bielsko, Poland. When the war began, she was living in Ptock, but she traveled to Vilna and joined the left-wing Zionist movement Ha-Shomer ha-Tsa'ir. After the Vilna ghetto was destroyed and 40,000 Jews were killed, she turned to the armed resistance of the United Partisan Organization. She eventually fled into the Rudninkai forest to work with Jewish partisan units.

After Vilna was liberated, Korczak-Marla emigrated to Palestine on December 12, 1944, and lived in Kibbutz Eilon and Kibbutz Ein ha-Horesh with other ex-partisans. She took part in educational projects and the establishment of Moreshet—the memorial museum named for Mordecai Anielewicz—and the Holocaust studies centers at Givat Haviva and Yad Mordecai. She published *Flames in the Ashes* in 1964 and died in 1988.

**BIBLIOGRAPHY**

Kowalski, I. *Anthology of Armed Jewish Resistance, 1939–1945*. Vol. I. Brooklyn, N.Y.: Jewish Combatants Publishing House, 1986, pp. 484–85; EncHol.

## KUNTSEVITCH, SOPHIA

(1925–   )
**Soldier, Ukraine**

Sophia Kuntsevitch was born in 1925 in Heyko, a small town in western Byelorussia. She studied to become a teacher and graduated when she was sixteen years old. When World War II began, she volunteered for combat duty in the Ukraine but was told she was too young. She met a man outside the recruiting office who changed her identification card and three days later she tried again and was accepted. In December 1941 she was wounded in the stomach while pulling an injured man to safety. She was in a field hospital for three months and upon release begged to go back into combat. Officials accepted and sent her to the front line in southwest Ukraine. Three weeks later she was wounded again in the stomach and leg, but again returned to combat.

In 1942 she was part of a battle in the Caucasus Mountains. When the last officer was wounded, he put Kuntsevitch in charge and she led the attack. When reinforcements finally came, only she and forty of the entire division were left. She received the Order of the Red Banner for her part in the battle. That same year she was wounded a third time and was taken to a hospital in Armenia. Hospital authorities offered to send her to a medical institute in Moscow for further medical training, but she refused. They sent her back to the front and after advancing into Berlin she wrote on a pillar, "I, Sophia Kuntsevitch, Russian daughter of a welder, came here and defeated racism." Five days before victory, she was wounded again, this time in the liver, an injury that kept her in the hospital for all of 1946. Upon her release, she found her health had deteriorated so much that she did not have the stamina required to attend medical school, and she trained in library science instead. After the war she married a partisan who had fought in Byelorussia and they settled in Minsk.

## BIBLIOGRAPHY

Saywell, Shelley. "The Eastern Front: Soviet Union, 1939–45." In *Women in War*. New York: Viking Penguin Inc., 1985.

# KUTORGIENÉ-BUIVYDAITE, ELENA

(1888–1963)
**Rescuer, Lithuania**

Elena Kutorgiené-Buivydaite was born in Siauliai (until 1917, Shavli), Lithuania in 1888. She studied at Moscow University and in 1912 received a medical degree. She worked as an ophthalmologist in a Moscow hospital until 1922 when she returned to Kovno, Lithuania. She continued her career and worked with a Jewish welfare organization for children, Oeuvre de Secours aux Enfants. When the Germans invaded Lithuania, Kutorgiené began concealing Jews in her home and in various locations throughout the city. She also held meetings with local partisans

Elena Kutorgiené-Buivydaite. Yad Vashem Photo Archives, courtesy of
USHMM Photo Archives.

in her home. She and her son also helped obtain arms and distribute
anti-Nazi literature and she managed to hide the writings of Haim Yelin,
commander of the ghetto underground, in her home. When Kovno was
liberated in August 1944, Kutorgiené worked for the Special Government
Commission for the Investigation of War Crimes. She had kept a diary
during the war, and she eventually published excerpts in the USSR and
Israel. She received the Order of Lenin, the Medal for Work during the

Great Patriotic War, and the honorary title of Outstanding Doctor of Lithuania in 1958. In 1982 Yad Vashem named Kutorgiené a "Righteous Among Nations."

**BIBLIOGRAPHY**

EncHol.

# L

## LEIDER, FRIDA

**(1888–1975)**
**Opera Singer, Germany**

Frida Leider, one of Germany's foremost opera singers, was at the height of her career during the Third Reich. She was born on April 18, 1888, the daughter of a Berlin carpenter. She worked as a bank clerk to support her musical education and debuted as Venus in *Tannhauser* in 1915. By 1923 she was a member of the Berlin State Opera and for the next fifteen years traveled extensively as an international star. From 1924 to 1938 she made annual guest appearances at Covent Garden in London.

On December 8, 1928, she made her U.S. debut at the Chicago Civic Opera as Brunhilde in *Die Walkure*. She also appeared in Milan, Paris, Vienna, Stockholm, Brussels, Chicago, Buenos Aires, and Bayreuth, where the annual Wagner festival was performed. In 1933 and 1934 she appeared at the Metropolitan Opera House in New York. During the second season, she received a cool reception by some other performers who criticized her for continuing to appear at Bayreuth. That same year, Hitler canceled all leave for the United States. Leider was scheduled to appear for a third season at the Metropolitan Opera, but had to choose between America and Germany. She canceled her contract with the Metropolitan Opera.

In 1938, Leider's husband, violinist Rudolf Demian (sometimes spelled

Deman), automatically lost his Austrian citizenship when Germany annexed Austria. Leider was pressured to divorce her Jewish husband, but she refused and he managed to escape from Germany and took refuge in Switzerland for the next eight years. Leider remained in Germany to continue her career. However, as a member of the State Opera, she was allowed to travel to concerts in Switzerland and other major European cities and she and her husband were reunited during those visits. Her last public appearance was on January 16, 1946. After the war, from 1945 to 1952, she directed the first of the German opera studios. She described her experiences, including the time Russian troops took over her house in 1945 and dressed up in her wigs and costumes before driving away with her furniture, in her autobiography *Playing My Part*, published in 1966. She died on June 4, 1975.

**BIBLIOGRAPHY**

Ewen, David, ed. *Living Musicians*. New York: Wilson, 1957; Leider, Frida. *Playing My Part*. Trans. Charles Osborne. New York: Meredith, 1966; Sutcliffe, J. H. "Lady of Berlin." *Opera News*, January 28, 1967, 28–29; obituaries in NewYT, June 5, 1975, 40; *Opera*, August 1975, 733–37; *Opera News*, July 1975, 28; MusS 456–57; Scott, Michael. *Record of Singing*. New York: Holmes & Meir, 1980, 198–200; NewYTBS 75; InWom; NewEOP 71; Baker 78; BioIn 4, 7, 10, 11, 12; ConAu 57; AnnObit of 71.

# LUBETKIN, ZIVIA

**(1914–1976)**
**Underground Leader, Poland**

Zivia Lubetkin, a leader of the Jewish underground in Poland and a founder of the Jewish Fighting Organization, was born in Beten, Poland in 1914. She joined *Freiheit* (a Zionist pioneering youth movement) and was a member of He-Haluts Ha-Lohem's Executive Council. When World War II began, she returned to German-occupied Warsaw. She joined the underground, specializing in propaganda and arms smuggling. In 1942 she was one of the founders of the Anti-Fascist Bloc, the first group in the Warsaw ghetto to offer armed resistance against the Germans. In July she helped establish the Jewish Fighting Organization and was one of the five members of the Jewish National Committee responsible for political leadership. In January 1943 she participated in the armed resistance operation and in April she participated in the Warsaw Ghetto uprising, commanding a bunker during its final days. On

May 10 she left the bunker and traveled into the "Aryan" area of Warsaw by way of the sewers. She hid in the Warsaw underground until the end of the war.

After the war Lubetkin was active in the Sheerit ha-Peletah organization. In 1946 she moved to Palestine and was one of the founders of Kibbutz Lohamei ha-Getta (Ghetto Fighters Kibbutz) and its Memorial Center. She held public positions in the Kibbutz movement and was a witness at the trial of Adolf Eichmann.

### BIBLIOGRAPHY

Lubetkin, Zivia. *In Days of Destruction and Revolt*. Terre Haute: Indiana University, 1980; Syrkin, M. "Zivia: The Passing of a Heroine." *Midstream* 24 (October 1978): 56–59; GoodHS.

# LUBIN, GERMAINE

**(1890–1979)**
**Opera Singer, France**

Germaine Lubin, whose reputation was ruined by her collaboration with the Nazis, was one of the most important stars at the Paris Opera by the time she was thirty-two. While singing at the Opera, her co-star, Lauritz Melchior, returned to the Berlin Opera and brought her to the attention of the director Heinz Tietjen. In February 1938 she was invited to sing Sieglinde in Berlin. Her performance was acclaimed and she was asked to sing at the Bayreuth Festival. She became close friends with Winifred Wagner, wife of the famous composer Richard Wagner, and she met Adolf Hitler at Bayreuth. Although Lubin insisted she had never been interested in politics and considered canceling her engagement in Germany after the invasion of Czechoslovakia, she nevertheless continued to sing there. After the invasion of France, her son was taken prisoner and she used her influence to get him released. She was offered a chance to sing in America, but her exit visa was refused.

Although Lubin was said to have hidden people on her estate until they could escape to the unoccupied zone, in 1946, Lubin was called before a court of justice in Orléans on charges of fraternizing with the Germans and denouncing her French gardener and his wife so that they were shipped to Germany where the gardener died. She was released, and several similar episodes occurred. She later said, "except for having eaten the flesh of children, there is nothing I was not accused of." Rumors circulated that she had affairs with high-ranking Nazis such as Foreign Minister Joachim von Ribbentrop, Admiral Donitz, and Hitler; she was supposedly the godmother to Hermann Goering's children. When she visited the German embassy in Paris, they accused her of being a spy. She received anonymous letters and was dismissed from the Opera with no pension. She was condemned to "national degradation" (loss of civil rights) for five years, and could not live in or near Paris or Tours for twenty years. Her money was confiscated and she could not teach at any musical conservatory. The French government also denied her visas to sing outside France. In 1949 her trial was reviewed in Paris and the twenty-year "interdiction de séjour" was reduced to five years and her property restored. At that point she was living in one sparsely furnished room. In 1950 she began giving recitals again and coaching other artists. She died, acclaimed by the French press, in 1979.

### BIBLIOGRAPHY

Rasponi, Lanfanco. *The Last Prima Donna*. New York: Knopf, 1982, 86–97; Christiansen, Rubert. *Prima Donna: A History*. New York: Penguin Books, 1986, 281–82; "M. de Lubin Revisited." *Opera News*, January 22, 1966, 27; Rasponi, L. "Germaine Lubin." *Opera News*, April 5, 1980, 10–15; "Return of Lubin." *Newsweek*, April 10, 1950, 78; Ewen, David, ed. *Living Musicians*. New York: Wilson, 1957, 102–3; BioIn 2, 4, 6, 7, 14, 15; InWom; NewEOP 71.


## LUDENDORFF, MATHILDE

(    –1966)
**Author, Germany**


In 1934 Mathilde Ludendorff's book, *Redemption from Christ*, was banned by the Prussian government. Adolf Hitler approved the ban, claiming the book was offensive to Christians. Mathilde Ludendorff was the wife of General Erich Ludendorff, chief of staff of the German armies in World War I and an early supporter of Hitler.

Mathilde Ludendorff and her husband promoted the Tannenberg League, named for one of the General's World War I victories over the Russians. They became known for advocating a supernaturalist cult that was against all religions and philosophies of a "cosmopolitan character." They planned to replace traditional religions with all-Aryan pagan cults based on ancient Germanic folk gods. In 1938, at the Nazi Party Congress in Munich, she was able to discuss her philosophies on the danger of the Tibetan lamas infiltrating Germany from the Himalayas with Hitler. In 1939 the Nazis ordered her to cease publication of the Tannenberg's official newspaper and little was heard of her until after the war when, though she had never been a member of the Nazi party, she was arrested and charged with being a Hitler supporter. In 1949 West German officials banned the organization's meetings. In 1951 she lost her property and civil rights and was sentenced to a year of "specially assigned work." In 1961 the organization itself was also banned in West Germany. Ludendorff died on May 14, 1966, in Tutzing, Germany.

### BIBLIOGRAPHY

Polgar, Alfred. "Two Ladies of the Regime." *Commentary*, June 9, 1950, 551–52; obituary in NewYT, May 15, 1966, 88; BioIn 2, 7.

## LUND, SIGRID HELLIESON

(1892–   )
**Resistance Worker, Norway**

Sigrid Hellieson Lund was born in Oslo, Norway, in 1892. Her father was a barrister and secretary of Norway's National Theater. At fifteen she was training to be a concert singer. In 1923 she became active in the Women's International League of Peace and Freedom and supported the Labor Party. In the 1930s, Lund helped political refugees from Nazi Germany and campaigned to free political prisoners in Germany. She sent money, letters of support, and packages to their families. In 1937 she lectured on pacifism and went to Czechoslovakia to rescue forty Jewish children. The group had to walk through Berlin streets because Jews were not allowed on trains and people spat at the children as they walked through the streets. Unfortunately, many parents asked that their children be returned to Czechoslovakia when Poland was overrun, and all the children went to the gas chambers.

   In 1940 Germany invaded Norway and Lund's entire family became involved in resistance work. Her sixteen-year-old son edited an underground newspaper; her husband, Diderich, coordinated activities, and Sigrid distributed funds, all activities that carried the death penalty. In September 1941 trade unionist leaders Viggo Hansteen and Rolf Wicstrom were arrested and shot. Lund was asked to take messages from the King and government-in-exile in London to Kirsten Hansteen, one of the widows. In 1942 Lund became more actively involved in the resistance movement with teachers Helga and Asta Sstene. When the quislings planned the Nazi Youth Organization, Lund and the Sstenes organized letters of protest from parents through underground channels throughout Norway. They collected thousands of letters and the ministry withdrew its plans.

After Lund's son was arrested and placed in Grini concentration camp, her home became a meeting place. When Claus Helberg, a commando from England, was sent to blow up a water plant needed by the Nazis for an atom bomb project, Lund aided his escape into Sweden. She became more active in arranging false papers and travel documents, finding hiding places, and picking up those in danger. On October 25, 1942, when a new law decreed that all Jewish men were subject to arrest, Lund spent the night warning as many people as possible. Hundreds escaped. She was also responsible for smuggling children in an orphanage into Sweden.

On January 27, 1944, after a visit by the Gestapo, Lund decided to try to escape. A month later, she and thirty-five other people walked for four to five hours to Sweden. She left one disabled son behind, the other in prison. She opened a small center for refugees and at the end of the war, when Scandinavian prisoners were released, she helped run a reception center at the port of Halsingborg; her own son, the editor, was among the prisoners.

After the war Lund became a Quaker and worked for the World Committee (FWCC). In 1945 she completed reconciliation work in Germany and two years later went to India to organize a kindergarten and health center. She became a member of the World Committee and in 1961 was executive chairperson of the European Section. She created the European Quaker Service, which was involved in a rehabilitation and development project in Kabylie, Algeria. The group rebuilt damaged schools and houses, provided water, and built and ran a mother-and-child-clinic. She was honored on her ninetieth birthday in 1982 for her global work in the social welfare field.

### BIBLIOGRAPHY

Sim, Kevin. *Women at War: Five Heroines Who Defied the Nazis and Survived*. New York: William Morrow and Company, 1982; Aarek, Hans Eirik, et al., eds. *Quakerism: A Way of Life. In Honor of Sigrid Hellieson Lund on Her 90th Birthday, February 23, 1982*. Kveker Forlaget, Norway: Norwegian Quaker Press, 1982.

# M

## MANN, ERIKA

(1905–1969)
Actress, Writer, Anti-Nazi, Germany

Erika Mann was born on November 9, 1905, in Munich, Germany to Kajja Pringsheim Mann and Thomas Mann, the novelist. She attended high school in Bavaria until she and her brother Klaus had to be transferred because of volatile relations with their anti-Republican classmates and teachers. They went to Heidelberg to continue their schooling.

Erika became an actress and married actor Gustaf Gründgens. When her husband became a Nazi she divorced him and continued her unconventional life. She won a 6,000 mile race through Europe sponsored by Ford and received a car that she later used to escape from Germany. In 1933 she wrote a political/literary review called *The Pepper Mill* that lampooned the Nazis. It played to capacity audiences until the Nazis stopped her from performing it and forced her to leave Germany because of her frank criticism of the Third Reich. On March 12, 1933; she left for Switzerland where her parents were vacationing. Erika convinced them it would be unsafe for them to return to Germany, even to pack their belongings. She returned home once to rescue her father's manuscript, the tetralogy *Joseph and His Brothers* (1933–1943). Other than the text, everything the Manns owned was left behind. They never returned to Germany.

Mann continued to perform *The Pepper Mill* in Holland, Switzerland,

Erika Mann. New York World-Telegram & Sun
collection.

Austria, Czechoslovakia, Belgium, Luxembourg, and New York. She
staged 1,043 performances before the review was barred due to German
government protests and a gas-bomb riot in Zurich. She also lost her
German citizenship. In 1935 Mann married the English poet and anti-
Fascist W. H. Auden, in what was later described as a marriage of con-
venience, and the two traveled to Europe. In 1936 she lectured in the
United States for four months. In 1938 she wrote *School for Barbarians,*
which described Hitler's effect on Germany's children. In 1939 she and

her brother Klaus wrote *Escape to Life*, which described German emigration. This was followed in 1940 by a series of lectures in the United States on Nazi Germany titled "The Other Germany." Mann was in London when Germany began bombing and she broadcast to the German people through the BBC. In 1940 she wrote another book, *The Lights Go Down*, which described the indignities of ordinary Germans under Hitler. In 1941 she was a guest at the White House. She and Klaus continued their protests until 1949, when Klaus died. She returned to Switzerland in 1950 to live with her aging father who died in 1955. Mann continued to write and died in Zurich on August 27, 1969, after surgery for a brain tumor.

### BIBLIOGRAPHY

Obituary in NewYT, September 29, 1969, 42; obituary in *Time*, September 12, 1969, 85; EncWT; EncTR; CurBio 40; AnnObit of 69; BioIn 4, 8, 9; ConAu 25R; InWom; TwCA; TwCA Supp.; CurBioYrbk 1969.

## MANSBACHER, HERTA

(1885–?)
**Schoolteacher, Resistance Fighter, Germany**

Herta Mansbacher, a Jewish schoolteacher who chose to stay in Germany with her students rather than flee to Egypt to live with a distant relative, was born in Darmstadt, Germany, on January 7, 1885, to Jacob and Lina Mansbacher. She received her teacher's license and obtained a position in the Westend School in Worms. She quickly gained a reputation for being a firm, but fair disciplinarian. A caring schoolteacher who often paid travel expenses for pupils, she also gave food and clothing to needy children. She visited the students' homes when they were ill or had suffered a death in the family. Mansbacher had been teaching for twenty-eight years when Hitler came to power in 1933 and was conducting class when a loud knock sounded on the classroom door. She went to the door, was asked to step outside, and the children never saw her again. She was dismissed that day because she was Jewish.

Mansbacher found employment in the Worms Jewish school and from 1936 to 1937 was acting head of the school. During this time she stressed to her pupils and their families the possibility of emigrating to other countries. Mansbacher refused to leave, having turned down an opportunity to leave for Egypt. She encouraged her students to learn trades they might find useful abroad and emphasized learning foreign languages. On the evening of November 9–10, 1938, the school suffered from the violence of Kristallnacht (night of broken glass). The next day Mansbacher was on the streets of Worms loading a wheelbarrow with furniture so she could reopen the school. When the Nazis arrested the Rabbi, she saved the synagogue's holy objects from the fires set by the Nazis, including thirty historic, priceless Torah scrolls. When the Nazis returned a second time to finish burning the building, she stood between them and the synagogue. Although several of the teachers had been placed in concentration camps, the school reopened with about thirty pupils.

Mansbacher quickly realized the importance of keeping a record of the many citizens of Worms who were leaving Germany and became the unofficial recorder of the Jewish exodus. Her secret list included a chronological list that also included family origins, relatives, professions, and country of destination. She eventually had more than 600 names on her list of emigrants and during 1941–42 she completed an index of names. Mansbacher was again given charge of the school and continued to teach although there were only fifteen students in the school. She purchased school supplies for the children even though Jews were discouraged from entering stores. The school was finally closed in the winter of 1940–41.

Mansbacher began traveling to Frankfurt each day to take a cooking course so she could help in the Jewish old-age home in Worms. In February 1942 she received word that she would be going on a "trip of unspecified length to an unknown location." On March 19 she and seventy-five Jews were taken to the Worms train station and put aboard a freight car. They were taken to Mainz and placed in a warehouse with more than 900 Jews until the next day when they left "for the East." They were taken to Pilaski, near Lublin, Poland. Mansbacher was never seen again.

**BIBLIOGRAPHY**

Huttenbach, Henry R. *Life of Herta Mansbacher: Portrait of a Jewish Teacher, Heroine and Martyr.* New York: Hermon, 1980.

# MASSING, HEDE

(1899–1981)
**Soviet Spy, United States**

Hedwig Tune was born in Vienna, Austria, in 1899. She studied acting and literature after emigrating to Germany in 1921 and worked as an actress from 1921 to 1924. She had married Gerhart Eisler, a German Communist, in 1919. After their divorce in 1923, she married Julian Gumperz, an American-born German publisher and writer who was also a Communist. They emigrated to the United States in 1926 and lived in New York City for two years. In 1928 they returned to Germany where she met Paul Massing, a Marxist scholar, who asked her to accompany him to the Soviet Union. There she was recruited into the espionage underground in Moscow. In 1930 she divorced Gumperz and married Massing. Posing as a writer, she became a courier for the Russian underground. In 1933 she organized border crossings into Czechoslovakia for German dissidents. After her husband was imprisoned in the Hubertshof concentration camp in Germany in 1933, Massing returned to the United States and lived there until her husband's release in 1937. She returned to Germany, and in November 1937 she and her husband were sent to Moscow, where they were interrogated for almost eight months about their activities during the war. After their release they were allowed to sail for the United States.

In 1948, Massing was called upon to describe her espionage activities to the Federal Bureau of Investigation. When Alger Hiss, a former State Department official who was accused of giving official documents to Whittaker Chambers, a courier for a communist spy group, was indicted by a federal jury in 1948, Massing testified that he was a spy and Hiss was convicted of perjury and sent to prison. In 1950, Massing published an eighteen-part autobiography, *I Spied for the Soviet Union*, in newspapers in America, Great Britain, and Europe. In 1951 she published *This Deception*, an expanded version of the newspaper autobiography. She died of emphysema on March 8, 1981, in New York City.

**BIBLIOGRAPHY**

Massing, Hede. *This Deception*. New York: Duell, Sloan and Pearce, 1951; obituary in *National Review*, April 17, 1981, 405; obituary in NewYTBS, March 1981, 349; AnnObit of 81; ConAu 108; BioIn 2, 12.

# MAUERMAYER, GISELA

**(1914–   )**
**Athlete, Nazi, Germany**

Gisela Mauermayer, who won a gold medal in the 1936 Olympics for the discus event, was discovered by Adolf Hitler's Olympic talent scouts and given the opportunity to train under government coaches for a year prior to the Olympics. Hitler had made it state policy to produce gold medal winners for the 1936 Olympics to show Aryan superiority. She won the gold medal and after the Olympics began a teaching job in Munich.

When the Allies occupied the city, her home was robbed of all her medals and trophies. She lost her teaching job because of her Nazi party membership. After the war, Mauermayer earned her doctoral degree by studying the social behavior of ants at the Zoological Institute of Munich University. She remained single and lived with her sister while working as a librarian for the Munich Zoological Society.

### BIBLIOGRAPHY

Johnson, W. "After the Golden Moment." *Sports Illustrated*, July 17, 1972, 34+; BioIn 9, 10.

## MAYER, HELENE

**(1910–1953)**
**Athlete, Germany**

Helene Mayer, one of the greatest women fencers of all time, was born on December 12, 1910, in Offenbach, Germany, to Christian Mayer and Ludwig Karl Mayer, a Jewish doctor. From an early age, Mayer excelled in riding, swimming, skiing, and fencing. In 1923 she became the Women's Fencing Champion of the Weimar Republic. In 1928 she achieved international success in London and won a gold medal in foils at the Olympic Games in Amsterdam. She also won the National Championship in Italy and was received by Benito Mussolini. When she entered the International Fencing Tournament in Offenbach in 1929, she won all the events. In 1930 she won the German Championship in foils in Mainz, but did not participate in the European championship in 1931 because of the death of her father. She finished in fifth place at the 1932 Olympics in Los Angeles. Propaganda Minister Joseph Goebbels promoted Mayer as a national heroine and an example of perfect Nordic womanhood until he found out she had a Jewish father and Jewish grandparents. She was then expelled from the Offenbach Fencing Club. She returned to the United States and settled in California to study international law at the University of Southern California.

In 1936, despite her Jewish background, German Olympic officials invited Mayer to participate in the Berlin Olympics on behalf of Germany.

Helene Mayer. AP/WIDE WORLD PHOTOS.

Her participation created a furor when she gave the Nazi salute from the rostrum after winning a silver medal, while also wearing the white German uniform complete with swastika. Mayer's actions caused a great deal of speculation about why she participated, but she never divulged the reason. Some theorized that it was the only way she could defend her title. Others said that she wanted to see her family still living in Germany, or that the Nazi's threatened her family's safety if she did not participate. After the 1936 Olympics Mayer returned to the United States and won the U.S. Women's National Fencing Championship a total of eight times and became a United States citizen. She married a Stuttgart engineer in 1952 and returned to Germany, but died October 15, 1953, after a long illness.

**BIBLIOGRAPHY**

WhoWNG; obituary in NewYT, October 16, 1953, 27; obituary in *Time*, October 26, 1953, 97; AnnObit of 79; EncTR; BioIn 3.

## MEED, VLADKA PETEL

**(1921–   )**
**Resistance Fighter, Poland**

Vladka Meed was born in Warsaw, Poland, on December 29, 1921, to Shlomo and Chana Antosiewcz Petel. She was working as a dressmaker when she was forced to live in the Warsaw ghetto in 1942. She escaped by leaving with a group of workers. She established contact with sympathetic non-Jews and made arrangements for living quarters for other escaping Jews. Meed began making regular trips into the ghetto by climbing over a wall or bribing sentries. She took in money, letters, and illegal Polish literature and began rescuing Jewish children. Her life consisted of constantly being on the move, sleeping on floors, and staying everywhere from small apartments to a lime factory.

Meed began collecting arms, including dynamite, to smuggle inside. She and a coworker found a formula for making small bombs and Meed collected the chemicals potash, hydrochloric acid, and cyanide, added sugar and gasoline, and mixed the ingredients in secret. She delivered sticks of dynamite wrapped in greasy paper to look like food on the eve of the ghetto uprising. As she went over the ghetto wall the people helping her pulled the ladder away in a panic and Meed was left stranded until she was rescued by her contacts who hid her under feathers and bedclothes until she could climb back over the wall. She was unable to get back into the ghetto and watched from a nearby room while the Nazis gunned down men, women, and children as they tried to escape.

In 1943 Meed's room was searched and Polish police arrested her and prepared to turn her over to the Gestapo, however, the police were bribed and they released her. That summer she was given a mission to travel to where a small group of insurgents from the Czestochowa ghetto were hiding. She made contact and went every few weeks taking money, clothes, and medicines.

In August 1944, Meed, feeling she was no longer effective or necessary, decided to leave the city. The following year she married Benjamin Meed and had two children, Anna, born in 1948, and Steven, born in 1951. She recounted her experiences in a book called *On Both Sides of the Wall* (1948). The book was published in Yiddish, Hebrew, Spanish, and English editions. The Meeds founded the Ben and Vladka Meed Registry of Jewish Holocaust Survivors at the United States Holocaust Memorial Museum and were integral in establishing the museum.

### BIBLIOGRAPHY

Meed, Vladka. *On Both Sides of the Wall: Memoirs from the Warsaw Ghetto*. New York: Educational Committee of the Workmen's Circle, 1948; Laska, Vera, ed. *Women in the Resistance and in the Holocaust: The Voices of Eyewitnesses*. Westport, Conn.: Greenwood Press, 1983; WhoAmJ.

## MEITNER, LISE

(1878–1968)
Scientist, Germany

Lise Meitner, called "our own Marie Curie" by Albert Einstein, was born on November 7, 1878, to Phillip Meitner, a lawyer, and his wife, Hedwig Skovan Meitner. Her parents were of Jewish background, but they baptized their eight children and raised them as Protestants.

Meitner was interested in physics at an early age, but her parents encouraged her to major in French so she could obtain a teaching position. In 1901 she entered the University of Vienna and began studying science instead. In 1905 she became the second woman to receive a doctorate in science from the University of Vienna with a dissertation on heat conduction in nonhomogenous materials.

After graduation Meitner became interested in radioactivity and designed and performed one of the first experiments that demonstrated that alpha rays were slightly deflected when passing through matter. She moved to Berlin in 1917 to study with the famous physicist Max Planck and met Otto Hahn with whom she worked for almost her entire professional life. Hahn needed a physicist to help him in his work on the chemistry of radioactivity, but he was working at the Chemical Institute under Emil Fischer who did not allow women in his laboratory. Hahn and Meitner set up their own laboratory in a carpenter's workshop and for two years carried out experiments there until Fischer succumbed and allowed Meitner in his lab. Still, because of her gender, she was not allowed to become a *Privatdozent* (at the time, an unpaid lecturer) but was made an assistant at the Institute for Theoretical Physics at the University of Berlin. In 1912 she transferred to the new Kaiser-Wilhelm Institute for Chemistry in Berlin–Dahlem. During World War I, the Hahn–Meitner experiments were curtailed when Hahn was called into service and Meitner volunteered as an X-ray technician with the Austrian Army at City Hospital in Lichterfelde, outside Berlin. The two scientists continued their experiments when their leaves coincided and by the end of the year they had identified the precursor of actinium called protactinium.

By 1926 Meitner had been appointed extraordinary professor and was working on clarifying the relationship between beta and gamma rays. She also developed a theory on how electron lines were generated from the outer electron shell, although the transition was named for Pierre Auger who described the process two years later in a different context.

In 1933 Adolf Hitler came to power, and although Meitner had never concealed her Jewish origins, she remained unaffected until April 7, 1933, when the Law for the Restoration of the Professional Civil Service (*Gestz zur Widerherstellung des Berufsbeamtentums*) was enacted. Non-Aryans, defined as anyone having at least one Jewish grandparent, were to be purged from government agencies, including universities. Meitner was concerned, but thought she would be safe because the university was not government-controlled, she had served in World War I, and she had been baptized as a Protestant. Nonetheless, she was required to fill out a questionnaire indicating her war service and, for the first time in her life, the question of utmost importance to the Nazi party—the *Rassezugeborigkeit der Grofseltern* or racial membership of her four grandparents—was asked. Still, Aryan friends and colleagues encouraged her not to resign despite the fact that most of her Jewish colleagues had fled or been dismissed and replaced by pro-Nazi scientists. The German Students Association became active on campus, burning books and demanding the dismissal of all Jewish personnel. Nearly one-third of Berlin's physicists were dismissed. Meitner's name appeared on a list of faculty to be dismissed and on September 6, 1933, her *venia legendi* (right to teach) was rescinded. This had no direct effect on her laboratory work or salary, but she was unable to teach or take on new doctoral students, attend the Wednesday physics colloquium, or give reports at scientific meetings. The next year a young lecturer tried to bring charges against her but failed, and by 1936 even her name was suppressed. In 1938 Kurt Hess, an avid Nazi colleague, denounced her as a danger to the Institute whereupon Hahn withdrew much of his support for Meitner in fear of retaliation both on him and the Institute.

Meanwhile, friends from outside Germany were begging Meitner to leave. They tried to find her another position and took up collections so she would have money to live on until she could resume her career. Her visa had expired to travel outside the country, and she frantically tried to get it reinstated. In so doing, she attracted the attention of Heinrich Himmler and her position became even more urgent. In July 1938, the Dutch physicist Peter Debye arranged for her to enter Holland and Dick Costner, another physicist, smuggled her out of Germany. Meitner was given an hour and a half to pack. She had two suitcases of summer clothes, ten marks, and a diamond ring belonging to Hahn's mother when she and Costner took a train to the border. They managed to evade SS passport control searches of trains. Dutch immigration officials allowed her to enter the country without a visa and with a worthless Austrian passport.

Meitner traveled from Holland to Denmark and eventually resumed her career at the Nobel Institute in Stockholm where scientists were constructing a cyclotron. At sixty years old, she had to learn a new language, organize a new research group, and start publishing papers again. Using Einstein's mass-energy equivalence, the team of Hahn, Fritz Strassman, and Meitner had determined that a large amount of energy would be released; they called this energy "nuclear fission." When they published the discovery, however, it was done under the names of Hahn and Strassman and the Nobel Prize was awarded to Hahn alone. Meitner was invited to join a team working on the development of the nuclear bomb, but refused.

Meitner published more than 140 scientific papers during her career and in 1946 she was invited to lecture as a visiting professor at Catholic University in Washington, D.C. She retired from the Nobel Institute in 1947 and worked in a small laboratory at the Royal Academy for Engineering Sciences in Sweden. In 1959 she returned to the United States to lecture at Bryn Mawr College in Pennsylvania. In 1960 she moved to Cambridge, England, where she died on October 27, 1968, a few days before her ninetieth birthday. Her tombstone reads, "Lise Meitner: A physicist who never lost her humanity."

## BIBLIOGRAPHY

Hahn, Otto. *A Scientific Autobiography*. New York: Charles Scribner's Sons, 1966; Sime, Ruth. *Lise Meitner: A Life in Physics*. Berkeley: University of California Press, 1996; Crawford, Deborah. *Lise Meitner, Atomic Pioneer*. New York: Crown Publishers, 1969; Watkins, Sallie. "Lise Meitner's Scientific Legacy." In *Making Contributions: An Historical Overview of Women's Role in Physics* (25–41). Katherine R. Sopka et al., eds. College Park, Md.: American Association of Physics Teachers, 1983; "Dr. Lise Meitner." *Nature* 162, no. 6 (1948): 726–27; Walz, J. "Her Specialty: Atoms." *New York Times Magazine*, March 10, 1946, 56; Silman, R. "Atom Age Mona Lisa—Dr. Lise Meitner." *Saturday Review*, June 6, 1959, pp. 52–54; Yost, Edna. *Women of Modern Science*. New York: Dodd Mead and Company, 1959; obituary in NewYT, October 28, 1968, 1; obituary in *Newsweek*, November 11, 1968, 97; obituary in *Time*, November 8, 1968, 86; Frisch, O. R. "Lise Meitner." In *Biographical Memoirs of Fellows of the Royal Society*. London: Royal Society of London, 1970; Watkins, Sallie A. "Lise Meitner, 1878–1968." In Grinstein, Louise S., Rosie K. Rose, and Miriam H. Rafailovich, eds. *Women in Chemistry and Physics: A Bio-Bibliographic Sourcebook*. Westport, Conn.: Greenwood Press, 1993, 393–402; CurBio 45, 68; WhoAmJ 68; BioIn 1, 3, 4, 5, 6, 8, 9, 11, 12; GoodHS; HerW; InWom; IntDcWB; WhAm 5.

# MIKHAYLOVA, KATYUSHA

**(1926–   )**
**Soldier, USSR**

Katyusha Mikhaylova, the youngest of three orphaned children, was on a train on June 22, 1941, at Smolensk, Soviet Union, when it was bombed. The fifteen-year-old was one of the few people in the train to survive. She made her way to military headquarters to volunteer and even though she had obtained a Red Cross certificate allowing her to volunteer, they told her she was too young. She managed to volunteer at a nearby hospital when she met a commander of a rifle unit who was desperate for medical personnel and let her enlist. She marched thirty miles a day on her way to Moscow to defend the city and slept in ditches and suffered from bleeding feet. A high-explosive shell hit her while on the march and destroyed the shinbone of her left leg. She was told the leg would have to be amputated, but after she told the doctor she would consider suicide rather than lose a leg, he decided not to operate. She was evacuated to a sanitarium in the coastal city of Baku and recovered with only a limp.

Mikhaylova volunteered for combat duty again and in the summer of 1942 was stationed on a naval hospital ship on the Volga River, loading the wounded. The ship was bombed and sank and Mikhaylova was rescued from the sea. When the battle of Stalingrad took place in February 1943, she volunteered to enlist in a newly formed Marine unit and again she was rejected. She wrote to the Naval High Command in Moscow and they allowed her to enlist. When she reported for duty, the other sailors presented her with a baby's pacifier. She was the only woman in the battalion and received the same training as the men, including a fifty kilometer march and training in amphibious landings. She carried hand grenades, antitank grenades, machine-guns, and a medical bag. Her first operation was the capture of Temryvk. After the battle, she received an apology from her fellow Marines for their previous treatment of her.

Mikhaylova received the Order of the Patriotic War for her actions in one of the largest amphibious landings and attack on Kerch'El'tigen by Soviet marines. It began on October 31, 1943, and ended on December 11. In December 1944 she helped storm the fortress of Iluk in Yugoslavia. The island was mostly underwater and she had to swim with bullets flying overhead. She was shot in the shoulder, but used an antitank grenade and her machine gun to kill fifty-six Germans. She was taken to the hospital in Novisad with twenty-two bullet fragments in her shoulder and pneumonia from the icy water. She was recommended for the title of Hero of the Soviet Union, but Moscow generals refused to believe the commander's description of the events and she did not receive the award.

After the war Mikhaylova became a doctor, settled in Moscow, and became active in the Women's Association for Peace.

## BIBLIOGRAPHY

Saywell, Shelley. "The Eastern Front." *Women in War* (130–58). New York: Viking Penguin, Inc., 1985.

## MUSU, MARISA

(1925–   )
**Partisan Fighter, Italy**

In 1940 at the age of fifteen, Marisa Musu began attending Communist Party meetings with Carla Capponi, a twenty-year-old translator, and worked as a liaison agent. She helped coordinate the activities of other protest groups such as the Socialists, the Action Party, and the Christian Democrats. She disseminated subversive literature and organized public demonstrations and strikes. When the Germans invaded Rome Musu became a member of the Gappisti or GAP (Groups of Partisan Action) and without any training participated in disruptions of the German occupation forces.

On December 18, 1943, Musu participated in her first armed action with Carla Capponi when they attacked a Fascist commander. They were also together in the bombing of an opera house. She took part with three others in a plan to assassinate Vittorio Mussolini, Benito Mussolini's son. However, police were waiting for them at the Mussolini home and they were captured not as partisans but, mistakenly, as thieves. While she was in jail, a former GAP member approached her parents and threatened to expose her as a partisan if they did not pay him. Her father refused and she was identified as a partisan. Meanwhile, plans were being made for her rescue. She was to pretend to have appendicitis and the chief of the jail, who supported the GAP, would see to it that she was taken to a hospital. A doctor who was also a partisan would pretend to operate and then help her escape at night. Unfortunately, the doctor was not on duty that day and there was no room at his hospital, so she was taken to another hospital and prepared for surgery. She finally confessed to the head surgeon and was returned to the ward. The partisans convinced the policeman guarding her to join their ranks and Musu escaped. She was taken to a convent where she stayed until the Americans entered Rome on June 1, 1944. On June 4 she returned home, married the GAP commander, and pursued a career in journalism. She received the Silver Medal for Military Valor.

### BIBLIOGRAPHY

Saywell, Shelley. "Via Rasella: Italy, 1939–1945." In *Women in War*. New York: Viking Penguin Inc., 1985.

# N

## NEURATH, IRMAGARD VON

(?–1965)
**Resistance Worker**

See Neurath, Wendelgard Von.

## NEURATH, WENDELGARD VON

(1925–   )
**Author, Resistance Worker, Germany**

Wendelgard von Neurath, who wrote an account of her mother's anti-Nazi activities, was born in Heidelberg, Germany, in 1925 to Baron Ernst von Neurath and his wife Irmagard. Despite their aristocratic background, the family cared for Russian prisoners in World War I. After reading Marxist literature Irmagard became a Socialist. Irmagard was also the niece of Hitler's first foreign minister, Constantin von Neurath, although the families had little to do with each other because of her "peculiar views."

In 1933 Wendelgard von Neurath attended Hitler Youth meetings although she was too young to join. Her mother considered going abroad, but did not want to lose the house and farm where they lived in a small village near Stuttgart. She appeared at the evening meetings of the Nazi Women's Corps as required, but predicted there would be a war that would destroy the country. When war did break out, she withdrew from all party activities. She told prisoners of war working on the farm—Poles, Frenchmen, and Russians—that there would be no war on her farm. Meanwhile, Irmagard's husband was drafted into the District Army Command and her son, a diabetic, joined the Northern Volunteer Legion of the Waffen SS. Wendelgard went to school in Berlin, then to an agricultural training farm that enemy planes often strafed.

In July 1944 Wendelgard von Neurath returned home and found a camp under construction in nearby Vaihingen meadows. It was rumored to be a factory where a new kind of aircraft would be produced. Soon however, she and her mother realized it was really a concentration camp for Jewish prisoners who were transported from Camp Wiesengrund. Her mother concocted a plan to help them despite her father's protests. Von Neurath and her mother called on the camp commandant. They agreed that the prisoners could come to the farm to pick beans and that there would be no beatings. Irmagard fed them sausages and bread, potatoes, and cottage cheese. Slowly, the prisoners grew stronger and the sores caused by malnutrition began to heal. She also concocted a plan whereby prisoners could work in the farm's greenhouse. When she found a prisoner with typhus, she put him in a small room in the greenhouse to rest each day to prevent his being shot by the guards.

In 1945 the Americans were advancing on the construction site and the von Neuraths feared the Nazis would kill all the prisoners. With permission from the camp commandant, the von Neuraths, Irmagard and Wendelgard, hid as many prisoners as possible in nearby shafts that were supposed to be used as underground runways. The two women supplied food so the prisoners could hold out against the SS guards if necessary. They brought straw for mattresses and sacks full of dried beans and peas. In addition, Irmagard sheltered a group of about twenty Russians in the greenhouse. When the Allies advanced further toward the village, Irmagard fashioned a huge banner that read "Here are 2,000 men in greatest depression. Come and help." Unfortunately, the prisoners were moved back to the camp and when they tried to find out why, Irmagard and Wendelgard were threatened with machine guns.

Irmagard eventually found out that the prisoners had been loaded into boxcars and that the commandant had prepared the shafts for the guards. They never moved the prisoners out of the village however, and when liberated, the prisoners took over the village. When the Americans arrived, Irmagard von Neurath was arrested. Wendelgard took the train to Stuttgart to contact a former prisoner named Jakob. He drew up a letter to the military government telling of the help that the von Neuraths had given them and got former prisoners to sign it. They sent the letter to Heidelberg. Irmagard was later released, but the military government claimed to have never heard of the letter. Eventually Irmagard was called to testify before a French military tribunal in Rastatt against the guards and the commandant from Camp Wiesengrund. The judge said, "You are one German who helped save civilization. You have acted honorably and with charity" (von Neurath, 161).

After the war Wendelgard von Neurath studied economics at the University of Tubingen, Ecole de Science Politique in Paris, and the University of Southern California in Los Angeles. She lectured on the concentration camp, and from 1955 to 1961 she was in the German foreign service stationed in Bern, Bonn, and Washington as First Secretary of the West German Embassy. In 1961 she married Berndt von Staden, the future West German Ambassador to the United States from 1973 to 1979. In the 1950s the von Neuraths sold the farm and in 1960 the baron died. Irmagard died five years later. Wendelgard chronicled her mother's war activities in a book titled *Darkness Over the Valley* in 1982.

### BIBLIOGRAPHY

"Growing Up in Nazi Germany: A Backward Look." *New York Times Book Service*, August 12, 1981, 1138–39; BioIn 12.

# NEVEJEAN, YVONNE

(?–1987)
**Rescuer, Belgium**

Yvonne Nevejean, who was said to have rescued up to 4,000 Belgian Jewish children, was contacted by the Comité de Défense des Juifs en Belgique (Committee for the Protection of Jews in Belgium) when deportations of the Jews began in 1942. She helped save children who had become separated from their parents because either their parents were in hiding or had been deported. She became head of ONE, the Oeuvre Nationale de l'Enfance (National Agency for Children). The agency was government subsidized and supervised children's homes throughout Belgium. Children would be placed in religious and lay institutions or in private homes. The agency sent nurses and social workers to collect the children and give them new identities and ration cards.

Nevejean was also instrumental in raising the funds needed to carry out this work. She contacted banks and the French government in exile in London to gain funds that could be parachuted into Belgium. Although au-

Yvonne Nevejean. Yad Vashem Photo Archives, courtesy of USHMM Photo Archives.

thorities arrested some members of the organization, Nevejean was never arrested and often intervened on the behalf of others who were arrested. In one instance, when the Gestapo transported the entire staff and the Jewish children being cared for in the Wezembeek children's home to the Michelen camp in Belgium, Nevejean obtained help from Queen Mother Elisabeth, who in turn obtained help from Leon Platteau of the Belgian Ministry of Justice to get the children released. Queen Mother Elisabeth, Leon Platteau and Yvonne Nevejean were all awarded "Righteous Among Nations" by Yad Vashem. Nevejean died in 1987.

BIBLIOGRAPHY

EncHol.

# NOETHER, EMMY

(1882–1935)
**Mathematician, Anti-Nazi, Germany**

Emmy Noether was born on March 23, 1882, in Erlangen, Germany, to Max Noether, a noted research mathematician and professor at the University of Erlangen, and Ida Amalia Kaufmann Noether. She planned to teach English and French and from 1900 to 1902 she studied foreign languages at the University of Erlangen. In 1903 she decided to specialize in mathematics instead and attended the University of Gottingen. Because women could not be admitted as regular students, she was a non-matriculated auditor at both universities. When she was finally admitted as a regular student in 1904 she returned to the University of Erlangen, receiving a Ph.D. summa cum laude in 1907. In 1915 university officials invited Noether to lecture at Gottingen but she could not be appointed a *Privatdozent* (at the time, an unpaid lecturer with *venia legendi*, the right to teach) until 1919, again because she was a woman. In 1922 Noether was named *nichtbeamteter ausserorcentlicher* Professor (unofficial associate professor), an honorary position. She received a modest salary provided through a *Lehrowftrag* (teaching appointment) in algebra. Noether taught at Gottingen from 1922 to 1933 except for a visiting professorship in Moscow in 1928–29 and Frankfurt in the summer of 1930. She became known as one of the world's foremost women mathematicians. She devised mathematical formulations for several concepts found in Einstein's general theory of relativity. Noether also became known for her work in twentieth-century theoretical physics, discounted the idea that women were incapable of theoretical advances, and made major contributions in abstract algebra. She wrote some forty-five research papers and worked closely with doctoral students, having such a marked influence on many who would become famous mathematicians themselves, that they termed her work the "Noether school of mathematics." In 1932 she received the 400-reichmark Alfred Ackermann–Teubner Memorial Prize for advancement of mathematical science "for her total scientific production." That same year, she was invited to be one of twenty-one speakers, and the only woman, to give a major address at the International Mathematical Congress in Zurich. Despite her achievements, she was never made *ordentlicher* Professor (full professor).

In January 1933 pro-Nazi students were very active at Gottingen. The German Students Association demanded that professors and students be screened "according to their guarantee of thinking in the German spirit." Of the four directors of physics and mathematics at Gottingen, three were Jewish. These three would resign or be placed on leave before the year was out. On April 2, 1933, Noether received a letter from the Nazis stating, "On the basis of paragraph 3 of the Civil Service Code of April 7, 1933, I hereby withdraw from you the right to teach at the University of Gottingen." Not only was she Jewish, but it was rumored that she was dangerous because at one time she had offered her apartment as a meeting place for a group of leftist students. Always more interested in scholarly topics than politics, Noether continued to meet with her mathematics group, including one student who arrived each time in an SA uniform.

Meanwhile, Noether worked to find employment in another country, realizing that for her own safety she would have to leave country, relatives, and friends. She eventually received a $2,000 stipend from the Rockefeller Foundation and spent the year 1933 lecturing and researching at Bryn Mawr College in Pennsylvania and at the Institute for Advanced Study at Princeton. She returned to Germany in 1934 but found very few former acquaintances still there and that her brother had fled to Siberia. Noether went back to Bryn Mawr, hoping that one day returning to her homeland would be safe. She died suddenly on April 14, 1935, after complications for surgery of a pelvic tumor.

**BIBLIOGRAPHY**

Brewer, James W., and Martha K. Smith, eds. *Emmy Noether: A Tribute to Her Life and Work.* New York: M. Dekker, 1981; Srinivasan, Bhama, and Judith D. Sally, eds. *Emmy Noether in Bryn Mawr: Proceedings of a Symposium Sponsored by the Association of Women in Mathematics in Honor of Emmy Noether's 100th Birthday.* New York: Springer-Verlag, 1983; Dick, August. *Emmy Noether, 1882–1935.* Trans. H. I. Blocher. Boston: Basel Boirkhauser, 1981; obituary in *New York Herald Tribune,* April 15, 1935, 12; Beyerchel, A. D. *Scientists Under Hitler: Politics and the Physics Community in the Third Reich.* New Haven: Yale University Press, 1977; Kass, Simon G., and Patricia Fannes eds. *Women of Science: Righting the Record.* Bloomington: Indiana University Press, 1990; Macksey, Joan, and Kenneth Macksey. *The Book of Women's Achievements.* New York: Stein and Day, 1976; Ogilvie, Marilyn B. *Women in Science: Antiquity Through the Nineteenth Century.* Cambridge, Mass.: MIT Press, 1986; Grenstein, Louise S., and Paul J. Campbell, eds. *Women of Mathematics: A Bio-Bibliographic Sourcebook.* New York: Greenwood Press, 1987; Herzenberg, Carole L. *Women Scientists: From Antiquity to the Present.* West Cornwall, Conn.: Locust Hill Press, 1986.

# P

## PERL, GISELA

(1905 or 1910–   )
**Physician, Camp Prisoner, Hungary**

Gisela Perl, a Hungarian gynecologist, was both an inmate and a physician at Auschwitz from 1944 to 1945. In March 1944 Perl, along with her parents, her husband, and her son, were seized by the Gestapo for undetermined reasons in her hometown of Sighet in what is now Rumania and taken to Auschwitz. Gisela Perl was the only one to survive. She and five other women doctors and four nurses were selected to operate a hospital ward in the camp, treating everything from injuries caused by torture to lice and rat bites. She often performed surgery without anesthetic.

Meanwhile, Josef Mengele, director of the hospital at Auschwitz, ordered officials to report every pregnant woman to him. He told Perl they were sending the women to another camp where better nutrition, including milk, would be available. When she learned they were taking the women to the research block to be used in experiments, then thrown into the crematorium, Perl vowed there would never be another pregnant woman in Auschwitz. "Gisi Doctor," as she was called, performed more than 3,000 abortions, usually at night on the dirty floor of a restroom using her bare hands. Her patients included Irma Grese, the dreaded matron of the hospital. At one point Mengele issued an order that pregnant Jewish women and babies were to be spared. According to her autobiography, Perl had 292 pregnant mothers in her ward when Mengele changed his mind and sent the women to the crematorium.

In January 1945, camp officials moved Perl to a camp near Hungary, then two months later to Bergen-Belsen. After liberation by the British, she remained in the camp until the fall then wandered around on foot searching for her family. Nineteen days later she discovered that her father had died shortly after his arrest, her husband had died shortly before liberation, and her teenage son had died in the gas chamber. Perl tried to commit suicide by swallowing poison and was taken to a convent in France to recuperate.

In the winter of 1947 she went to the United States where the Congress passed a special bill granting her permanent residence in the United States, praising her for her "simple humanity" in saving "the lives of more than 3,000 women." Others condemned her. One was Dr. David Deutschman of New York who was quoted in *Time Magazine* as saying, "There is no rational or moral justification for . . . the wholesale slaughter of infants . . . whether it be done by the brutal Nazis, or by a sentimental and well-meaning female medical personality" (p. 56). Despite the remarks, Perl began to tour the United States calling herself the "Ambassador of the Six Million." She wrote her autobiography in 1948 entitled *I Was a Doctor in Auschwitz*. Eleanor Roosevelt encouraged her to resume her career in medicine and she joined the staff of Mount Sinai Hospital under Dr. Alan F. Guttmacher, the family planning pioneer, and opened her own office in Manhattan. She delivered thousands of babies and she also became an expert in treating infertility.

In 1979 Perl moved to Israel to fulfill a promise made to her father when the cattle-car doors were opened at Auschwitz, that they would one day meet in Jerusalem. She and her daughter, Gabrilla Krauss Blattman, who had been hidden by a non-Jewish family during the war, were last known to be living in Herzilya, Israel.

## BIBLIOGRAPHY

Perl, Gisela. *I Was a Doctor in Auschwitz*. New York: International Universities Press, 1948; NewYTBS 82; "Not So Simple," *Time*, September 20, 1948, 56–57; BioIn 1.

# POPOVA, NADYA

(?–?)
**Combat Pilot, USSR**

When Moscow was attacked in 1941 by Germany, three all-women regiments were formed—fighters, short-range bombers, and night bomber
units. Nadya Popova was one of the first to volunteer, even though she
was only nineteen years old. She was sent to aviation school in Hershol,
Ukraine, and during her first two weeks there her brother was killed.
Air Force authorities stationed her at a military air base near Saratov on
the Volga River. She trained on three classes of planes fourteen hours a
day, but specialized in U-2 light planes (night bombers) for the 588th
night-bomber regiment. Her first combat mission was near the southern
front in Ukraine. After that she flew combat missions across the Don
River with three hundred kilos of bombs strapped to the plane's wings.
Although thirty-three women of the 588th died, Popova continued to fly
until the end of the war.

**BIBLIOGRAPHY**

Saywell, Shelley. "The Eastern Front: Soviet Union, 1939–45." *Women in War*
(130–58). New York: Viking Penguin Inc., 1985.

# PORTEN, HENNY

(1890–1960)
**Silent Film Star, Germany**

Henny Porten was born in Magdeburg, Germany, on January 7, 1890.
Her father was an actor and she soon became a silent film star. One of
her films, *The Daughters of Kohlhiesel*, won worldwide acclaim. She and
Carl August Froelich formed the Porten–Froelich production company
just as sound was introduced, and it was very successful. Then in 1943
Hermann Goering demanded that Porten divorce her Jewish husband,
Wilhelm von Kaufmann-Aser, a physician, because the Nazis had clas-
sified Kaufmann-Aser as "non-Aryan." She refused and began a twelve-
year battle with the Ministry of Propaganda. During that time she had
only one major role. On February 14, 1944, her home was bombed and
she had nowhere to go, since sheltering homeless Jews was illegal. Even

after the war, Porten's career was never revived. She died on October 15, 1960, at age seventy, just a few hundred yards from the theater where she had begun her career as Gretchen in *Faust*.

**BIBLIOGRAPHY**

Obituary in NewYT, October 17, 1960, 29; BioIn 5; OxFilm; WhoHol.

# R

## REIK, HAVIVA

(1914–1944)
**Resistance Fighter, Slovakia**

Haviva Reik was born near Banska Bystrica, Slovakia, in 1914. She joined the Ha-Shomer ha-Tsa'ir Zionist youth movement, then moved to Palestine in 1939 to live in Kibbutz Ma'anit. She served in a strike force, then volunteered to join a parachutists' unit. On September 21, 1944, using the code name "Emma," she parachuted into Slovakia to contact the Procovna Skupina (Working Group), which was involved in the Slovak National Uprising led by Rabbi Michael Dow Weissmandel and Gisi Fleischmann. They were besieged by the Germans and therefore could do little to help the Jews. Banska Bystrica fell in October 1944, and Reik and the Working Group fled into the Tatra Mountains with a Jewish partisan group. They set about organizing a camp and collecting weapons. Six days later they were captured by a unit of the Ukrainian "Galicia" Waffen SS division. Reik was executed on November 20, 1944, at Kremnica.

After World War II, a kibbutz, an immigration ship, and an Israeli educational center were all named after Haviva Reik.

### BIBLIOGRAPHY

Benkler, R. "Haviva Reik: Heroine without Heroics." *Israel Horizon* (December 1964): 15–19; EncHol.

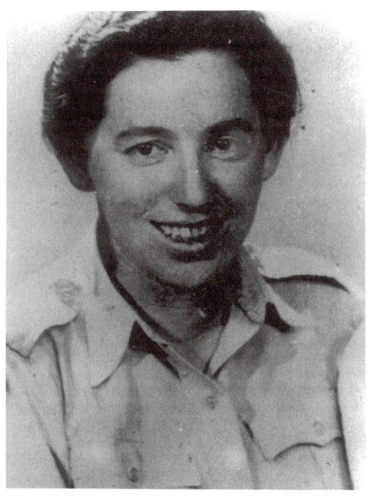

Haviva Reik. Moreshet Archives, courtesy of USHMM Photo
Archives.

## REISS, JOHANNA DELEEUW

(1932–  )
**Hidden Child, Author, Holland**

Johanna DeLeeuw was born in 1932 in Winterswijk, Holland, near the
German border. In 1942 her father, a cattle dealer, began making plans
for him and his three daughters to go to the homes of sympathetic Dutch

Christians. In October, when the family was ordered to a Dutch work camp, he placed the family in non-Jewish homes surrounding Winterswijk; their mother was in the hospital. Johanna and her sister Sini were sent to Usselo to live with a family named Hannink. During this time, their mother died and was hurriedly buried; the children were not allowed to attend the funeral for fear they would be arrested. Not long afterwards, the Hanninks were suspected of harboring fugitives and the girls were moved to another farmhouse with a family by the name of Oosterveld. Johanna and Sini were instructed to keep away from the windows and were kept inside with no exercise and no contact with other people. From 1943 to 1945 they lived in a tiny upstairs room. When the war ended in the summer of 1945, they walked outside for the first time. They were returned to their father and sister who educated Johanna in Holland where she taught school before emigrating to the United States.

In the late 1960s, Reiss took her two daughters to Usselo to see where she had lived during the war. In 1972 she put her experiences in a book for children called *The Upstairs Room*. It won the Charles and Bertie G. Schwartz Juvenile Award from the Jewish Book Council (1972); the Newbery Medal Honor Book Award (1973); and the Buxtehuder Bulle Outstanding Children's Book for Promoting Peace Award (1976). It was followed by *The Journey Back* in 1976.

**BIBLIOGRAPHY**

Reiss, Johanna. *The Upstairs Room*. New York: Bantam, 1972; Reiss, Johanna. *The Journey Back*. New York: Cromwell, 1976; "Memories of Childhood." *Saturday Review*, June 12, 1976, 8; Roginski, Jim, comp. *Newbery and Caldecott Medalists and Honor Book Winners: Bibliographies and Resource Materials Through 1977*. New York: Libraries Unlimited, 1983; AuBYP Supp.; TwCW 78B; SmATA 18, 250–53; HerW; ConAu 85; BioIn 15.

# REITSCH, HANNA

(1912–1979)
Pilot, Nazi, Germany

Hanna Reitsch was born on March 29, 1912, in Hirschbeerg, Silesia (occupied by Germany from 1939–45) to Willy Reitsch, a doctor, and Emy Reitsch. Her father had hoped she would become a doctor and in 1931,

Hanna Reitsch. Courtesy of the National Archives.

to encourage her to pass the Abitur, the school-leaving examination, he promised she could have a course of gliding lessons at a nearby school.

Reitsch was a natural aviatrix and in 1932 obtained her gliding- and powered-flying licenses. She immediately set a woman's endurance gliding record by staying in the air for five-and-a-half hours. She did attend medical school in Berlin, but spent most of her time at the flying school at Staaken, hoping to obtain a license to fly powered sports aircraft. In 1933 she set an unintentional altitude record when she was accidentally sucked into a thunderstorm.

Reitsch was invited to become an instructor at a new gliding school in Swabia. School officials asked her to join an expedition to South America in 1934 that she financed by accepting an offer from a film company, UFA, to act as a double in flying sequences for the heroine of the film. In South America Reitsch became the first woman to receive a Silver Soaring Medal. She was also invited to join the Gliding Research Institute at Darmstadt, Germany, and was a member of a German gliding team sent to Finland to create interest in the sport. For her work in Finland, the Reich Air Ministry awarded her a decoration. In 1934 she was the only woman allowed to join the Civil Airways Training School that consisted of 150 men.

In 1935 Reitsch became a *Flugkapitan* (Flight Captain), a civilian title previously given only to eminent, male Lufthansa pilots. She was invited to join the elite group of military test pilots at Reschlin. In 1938 she visited the United States for the annual Cleveland air races and because she declared she was not interested in politics, was not a member of the rising Nazi party, and openly supported Jews and complained about their treatment, she was welcomed with little controversy. Upon her return to Germany, however, she found that once the war officially began, her status had changed. Reitsch was not allowed to join the combat troops, train, or even communicate with other glider pilots. She was allowed to test a petrol-tanker glider, a bed-of-ropes landing, a balloon cable-cutting device, and the Me 163 and the manned VI (both German fighter planes). She was involved in several crashes during this period. In 1940, when Hitler learned of one of her more serious crashes, she became the first woman pilot to be awarded the Iron Cross, Second Class. Two years later she suffered her most serious accident that resulted in skull fractures in six places, a displaced upper jawbone, a smashed nose, several broken vertebrae, and a severely bruised brain. Her near-death experience earned her an Iron Cross, First Class. After ten months of painful rehabilitation in a mountain hideaway, she was flying again, boosting the morale of troops on the Russian front. It was said her picture and newspaper clippings were pinned in the barracks of the troops. During this time Hitler also gave her permission to organize Operation Self-Sacrifice, a suicide mission, and she was sent to reconnoiter emergency landing-grounds for hospital planes.

On April 25, 1945, Reitsch was requested to accompany Gen. Ritter von Greim to Berlin, which was already occupied by Russian troops. Hitler had insisted on seeing the general in the Berlin bunker despite the fact that for two days, no aircraft had managed to fly into Berlin. The general was flying the plane when enemy fire penetrated the plane and a bullet struck his right foot. Reitsch took over the controls by stretching over his shoulder and seizing the throttle and stick. She landed the plane on a Berlin street and a group of men rescued the two and took them in a truck to Hitler's air-raid bunker. The general learned that he and Reitsch had risked their lives so that Hitler could tell him he was the Reich's new commander in chief of the Air Force. Three days later, Hitler insisted Reitsch and von Greim leave and the two flew out at night.

As the war came to a close, Reitsch continued to fly the general to meetings throughout Germany until she was finally admitted to a hospital for exhaustion and shock. Her father had shot her mother, sister, and three nieces and nephews before killing himself rather than having to face living under the Russians. Von Greim also committed suicide using a cyanide capsule, also given to those people remaining in Hitler's bunker.

The Americans eventually arrested Reitsch and advised her to emigrate to America or face imprisonment by American counterintelligence. Reitsch chose to stay and intended to commit suicide, but after seeing photographs of Dachau, she decided to spend her life trying to exonerate her country. The Air Force Intelligence Unit in the American zone took her into custody because she was a figure of importance in Luftwaffe research and aircraft testing, as well as one of the last people to have seen Hitler alive. She was the only woman among fifty or so political and military leaders detained. She was released in July 1946, but kept under surveillance. In December 1947, she was part of a de-Nazification hearing.

Reitsch spent most of her remaining years flying and trying to combat rumors about her part in the war. She wrote three autobiographies and often complained in print about her portrayal in movies such as *Operation Crossbow* (1965), *The Last Days* (1973) and *Test Pilot* (1979). She began working to rebuild the gliding movement in Germany, although she was refused visas to outside events until 1952, when she was allowed to go to Spain.

In 1955 Reitsch became Germany's gliding champion and in 1956 she won the international gliding championship in France. In 1957 she set a woman's altitude record, and in 1959 she was sent on an official mission to India where she took Nehru gliding and lunched with Indira Ghandi. In 1961 she was received at the White House by President John F. Kennedy as part of the international association Whirley Girls. (Reitsch was Whirley Girl no. 1 because she was the first woman ever to fly a helicopter.)

From 1962 to 1966 Reitsch founded and ran the National School of Gliding in Ghana, but was expelled after a political coup. She won the first international woman's helicopter championship in 1969 and the next year was given an honorary membership in the Society of Experimental Test Pilots in the United States. She continued to set records almost to her death. In 1978 she set another world gliding record, and in 1979 she set a world record flight in the United States before dying of a heart attack on August 24.

### BIBLIOGRAPHY

Piszklewicz, Dennis. *From Nazi Test Pilot to Hitler's Bunker: The Fantastic Flights of Hanna Reitsch.* Westport, Conn.: Greenwood Publishing Group, 1997; Lomax, Judy. *Hanna Reitsch: Flying for the Fatherland.* London: John Murray, 1988; EncTR; WhoWNG; NewYTBS 79; BioIn 2, 3, 5, 7, 12; InWom; ConAu 89.

# RICHARD, MARTHE

(1889–1982)
French Spy, France

Marthe Betenfeld was born on April 15, 1889, in Lorraine, eastern France. She suffered a troubled childhood and by age seventeen was in reform school. She escaped from the school and by 1912 had married an attorney, Henri Richer, and became one of the first French women parachutists and aviators. She knew how to use firearms and spoke several languages, including German. Her husband was killed in May 1916, during World War I, and she was recruited by military intelligence to contact Baron Hans von Krohn, the German naval attaché and espionage chief of Spain. The Germans recruited her as an agent, unaware that she was a French agent, and she pretended to join German intelligence. She was sent to France to obtain information on armament production and gave the Germans false information. Meanwhile, she obtained information on the German submarine U-52 for the French. The Germans also sent her to Argentina to deliver instructions for German agents and carry vials of a chemical designed to contaminate Allied grain. The instructions and chemicals were not delivered. She remained in Spain for two more years before returning to France, where she was awarded the Legion d'Honneur. Several books were published describing her exploits, and she wrote *I Spied For France* in 1935. A film was also made of her life entitled *Marthe Richard, Spy*, also in 1935.

When World War II broke out, Richard became active in helping Allied airmen who had been shot down to escape. She set up an underground operation to return them to safety. Since she was working at the Vichy Air Ministry, she was able to forge the documents she needed to get the pilots to safety. She also hid them in her apartment until she could arrange for safe passage out of France.

After the war Richard was elected to the Paris Municipal Council and was instrumental in passing an act which outlawed houses of prostitution. The law became known as the Richard Law. Richard died on February 9, 1982, in Paris.

**BIBLIOGRAPHY**

AnnObit of 82; BioIn 1; "French Ex-Spy Paris: La Skylark." *Newsweek*, March 18, 1946, 52–53.

## RIEFENSTAHL, LENI

(1902– )
**Film Director, Actress, Germany**

Helen Bertha Amalie (Leni) Riefenstahl, best remembered for her work in film for the National Socialist party, was born in Berlin, Germany, on August 22, 1902. Riefenstahl was the daughter of Alfred Riefenstahl, a wealthy Berlin merchant, and Bertha Scherlach Riefenstahl. Encouraged by both parents to be independent, Leni decided to pursue dancing. She enrolled in the famous Russian Ballet School in Berlin and eventually became a success on the German stage.

While recovering from a knee injury in 1924, Riefenstahl went to the theater and saw Arnold Fanck's "mountain film," *Der Berg des Schicksals (Peaks of Destiny)*. Riefenstahl later stated that it made such a strong impression on her that she became determined to leave the stage to work with Fanck in the Alps. (The "mountain film" genre embodied the Teutonic ideal of conquering nature and relating folktales.) Riefenstahl arranged to meet Fanck and worked with him on several films, learning everything she could about film-making techniques and directing.

Leni Riefenstahl. Courtesy of
the National Archives.

These films established her as a film star, but in 1930 she decided to
start directing her own films. She used all the knowledge she had
gleaned from Fanck to direct and star in her first film in 1931, *Das blaue
Licht (The Blue Light)*. She experimented with various techniques to create
effects that had previously been used only by large studios with large
budgets. For instance, she was the first to combine a red and green filter.
The movie was a success and won a gold medal at the Venice Film
Festival in 1932. Hitler, a fan of "mountain" genre films because of the
Teutonic heroism represented in them, arranged to see it.

In 1933 Riefenstahl made her second film with Fanck. *SOS Eisberg*,
another mountain film, established her in the industry. That year she
also made a short film of the 1933 Nazi Party congress, *Sieg des Glaubens
(Victory of Faith)*, and was seen for the first time in Hitler's company, but
she had not joined the party. Hitler chose Riefenstahl to produce a chronological film following the events of the 1934 Nazi Party congress at
Nuremberg. She was the only filmmaker allowed to create a work with-

out the supervision of Josef Goebbels, Hitler's minister of propaganda. *Triumph des Willens (Triumph of the Will)* premiered at the Ufa-Palast-am-Zoo in Berlin on March 28, 1935. She used the unusual technique of aerial photography, and the film became one of the most famous propaganda films to come out of the war. In May 1935, at the Festival of the Nation, she was presented with the National Film Prize. Riefenstahl's success brought her funding and worldwide recognition as a filmmaker.

Riefenstahl's second and final project for the National Socialists was another propaganda film, *Olympia*. In 1936 Germany hosted the Olympic games. The Nazi's anti-Semitic views and policies were becoming apparent to the outside world and Hitler decided he needed a film to promote Germany as a peace-loving, but strong nation. Critics noted that Riefenstahl produced one of the best mixes of propaganda and art ever presented, especially of a sports event; however, Riefenstahl denied that it was a propaganda film. She did, however, win an award for the film after using new techniques including underwater photography and aerial shots of the stadium from a balloon. A trip to America in 1938 to promote *Olympia* resulted in protests and boycotts by the film industry. She returned to Germany to make more films with her own company, but because of the war, production became impossible. Riefenstahl returned to her home in Kitzbühel.

In 1945 Riefenstahl was picked up by American troops in Kitzbühel. Lengthy testimony was elicited at the Seventh Army Interrogation Center about her participation in the National Socialist Party. In 1949 they declared her a "sympathizer" during the de-Nazification trials in Nuremberg. (This meant she was not a Nazi, but indirectly aided the Nazi government cause.) The decision was, and still is, greatly contested. She was blackballed from working in the film industry or participating in film festivals, but continues today to deny she knew anything about the Nazis' activities.

## BIBLIOGRAPHY

Deutschmann, Linda. *Triumph of Will: The Image of the Third Reich*. Wakefield, New Hampshire: Longwood Academie, 1991; Berg-Pan, Renata. *Leni Riefenstahl*. Boston: Twayne, 1980; Downing, Taylor. *Olympia*. London: BFI Publishing, 1992; Graham, Cooper C. *Leni Riefenstahl and Olympia*. Metuchen, N.J.: Scarecrow Press, 1986; Hinton, David B. *The Films of Leni Riefenstahl*. Metuchen, N.J.: Scarecrow Press, 1978; EncTR; WhoWNG; CurBio; ConAu X; NewYTBS 74; IntDcWB; OxFilm; WhoHol A.

# RUTKIEWICZ, MARIA KAMIENIECKA

(1917–  )
**Resistance Fighter, Poland**

Maria Kamieniecka Rutkiewicz was born in Warsaw, Poland, on August 22, 1917, to a middle-class family. Her elder brother and sister were sent to prison for activities in the Communist youth movement in the 1920s, and Maria joined the Communist Party while still in school. She, too, was arrested for organizing illegal meetings at her school. In 1938 she married Wicek Rutkiewicz, a Party activist, and when her husband was placed in a prisoner-of-war camp, she fled to the Russian-occupied portion of Poland. She asked to join a small group of Party members called the Initiative Group. Rutkiewicz was trained as a radio operator and as one of the "human torpedoes," was dropped into Poland on December 28, 1941, near the village of Wiazowna, about twenty miles outside Warsaw. In May 1942, after replacing her lost radio, she began sending messages back to Russia.

In the autumn of 1942, officials released Rutkiewicz's husband and she returned to Warsaw to work with him in the Resistance. On September 14, the Germans stormed her house, and she destroyed the radio as they burst into the room. They took her to 25 Szucha Avenue and interrogated her for seven days. Although she was pregnant with twins, she was beaten so badly that the supervisor did not recognize her and did not know which cell to put her in. She refused to divulge any information and was sentenced to death. They transported her to a solitary cell in the women's section of Paviak, a building inside the ghetto that was a clearing house for political prisoners. Dr. Krystya Ossowska, who had worked in the prison hospital since 1940, cared for her. On February 16, 1944, Rutkiewicz gave birth to a boy and a girl. News of the event reached the outside by way of an underground paper and brandy and cigarettes were given to the guards in hope that she would receive better treatment. Dr. Ossowska managed to smuggle a camera into the prison and take a photograph of herself, Rutkiewicz, and the twins to send to Rutkiewicz's husband, who had no idea where his wife was.

On July 31 the gates of the prison were opened and a horse and cart driven by Helena Danielewicz from the prisoners' aid organization, Patronat, entered the prison. They told the mothers to put their babies in the cart, but at the last moment, the Gestapo arrived and ordered the women in, too. They drove through the gates, where Rutkiewicz's sister was waiting outside to meet her. Dr. Ossowska was kept behind to care for those who could not leave, and on August 13, 1944, the Germans shot them all. Rutkiewicz left Warsaw to live with relatives near Cracow in south Poland. Her mother was dead, a brother was killed in battle in September 1939; another was in Auschwitz. Except for the photograph, her husband never saw his children; he died in Sachsenhausen concentration camp. Rutkiewicz eventually married Arthur Starewicz, a high-ranking Communist official, and worked for the Communist Party. In 1971 Starewicz became Polish Ambassador to the Court of Saint James, and they lived in London until 1978.

## BIBLIOGRAPHY

Sim, Kevin. *Women at War: Five Heroines Who Defied the Nazis and Survived*. New York: William Morrow and Company, 1982.

# S

## SALOMON, CHARLOTTE

**(1917–1944)**
**Artist, Germany**

Charlotte Salomon, who, despite a family history of suicide that hung over her, managed to paint hundreds of watercolors depicting the dramatic events of her lifetime, was born on April 16, 1917, in Charlottenburg, Germany. In 1921 her mother, Franze Grunwald Salomon, committed suicide, as did her mother's sister Charlotte before her. Charlotte, named for her aunt, attended Furstin Bismark School and when her father, a doctor, was fired in 1933, she left school. In 1935, however, she was allowed to enter the world-famous State Art Academy in Berlin. Three years later, her enrollment was annulled, probably because she was Jewish, despite the fact that it was believed she had great talent. In January 1939 she escaped to the French Riviera, and began more than 700 watercolors overlaid by written texts that she called an "artistic autobiography," titled *Life? or Theater?* In 1940 her grandmother committed suicide and Salomon took her grandfather to live in Nice. She stayed with him for a short while, then moved to the resort town of St. Jean Cap Ferrat where she painted in a one-room apartment. In 1942 a law was passed that foreign Jews had to present themselves to the authorities, and a year later in 1943 Salomon was forced to move back to Nice and live with her grandfather in the home of an acquaintance. Her grandfather died on February 12, 1943. On June 17, Salomon married Alexander Nagler and the two hid in the homes of friends. In September 1943 the Nazis arrested them and she was taken to Drancy a camp a few miles outside Paris; her husband was sent to Auschwitz. Salomon died in Drancy on January 1, 1944.

**BIBLIOGRAPHY**

Felstiner, Mary Lowenthal. *To Paint Her Life*. New York: HarperCollins Publishers, 1994; BioIn 12.

## SANSOM, ODETTE BAILLY

**(1912–  )**
**Resistance Fighter, France**

Odette Bailly was born on April 28, 1912, to Yvonne and Gaston Bailly in Amiens, France. Her childhood was uneventful except for her father's death in World War I in 1914 and a bout with blindness cured supposedly by an herbalist. In 1930 she married Roy Sansom, an Englishman, and moved to London where she and her three daughters and her mother-in-law were living when World War II broke out.

In the spring of 1942, Commander Rodney Slessor asked the English people to send him their vacation photographs to help the war effort. He studied the photographs to help map out the topography of European countries. Odette sent photographs of Boulogne and a division of the War Office known as "the Firm" contacted her. A representative explained the division's task was to organize and train a secret army in France. The organization was known to the public as FANY (First Aid Nursing Yeomanry). They recruited women to drive the senior officers around and run errands. After her mother-in-law's death, she placed her children in a convent and joined the SOE (Special Operations Executive). They trained her and she became "Celine" or "S.23." She was supposed to parachute into France, but after several mishaps with airplanes, she traveled by troopship to France. On November 2, 1942, she arrived in Cannes and became a courier. One of her responsibilities was to accompany her supervisors in inspecting airfields for Allied landings. She became a wireless operator for Captain Peter Churchill, one of the major players in the SOE in Annecy.

On April 16, 1943, the Gestapo arrested Sansom and placed her in Fresnes prison in Paris. On May 25 they transported her in a van called the Black Maria to 84 Avenue Foch for interrogation. She was given a meal of meat and potatoes and released. The next day she was arrested again, and after refusing to give her interrogators the information they needed, a red-hot poker was placed on her spine and her toenails were torn out, one by one. Her captors were starting on her fingernails when the interrogation was called off. Meanwhile Churchill, whom she falsely identified as her husband, had been placed in cell 220 in Fresnes prison. Several days later she was condemned to death for carrying messages. When she was returned to her cell a new sign had been placed on the door, a red mark in the shape of a cross, a signal that she would be executed. Thirteen more interrogations followed. Meanwhile Sansom began fashioning a communications system to other prisoners from her cell.

Sansom managed to contact Peter Churchill and also carried on communications with other women prisoners until she was moved to a new cell in the fall of 1943 when she became ill. She was allowed to shower for the first time since the previous April and shared a cell with other women for the first time. On February 14, 1944, Peter Churchill was taken away and Odette was alone in Fresnes. On May 12, 1944, she was ordered to Germany, after spending a year and four days in Fresnes. When she left Fresnes she was still under a death order.

Sansom traveled by train to Germany with seven other women, all members of the French Section of the British War Office. Ironically, Odette was the only one condemned to death and she was the only one who survived. The women were handcuffed together and under a heavy SS guard were taken to the train station, singing as they went. They were taken to Karlsruhe criminal prison. In mid-July, she was moved to Frankfurt, where she was placed in a cage until she was moved to Ravensbruck. At Ravensbruck she lived in a long, windowless room filled with the odors of sweat, dirt, menstrual blood, and human excrement. Her cell mates were about forty Ukranian women who spoke neither English nor French. Finally, on July 18, 1944, she was taken to the Ravensbruck prison itself and detained until April 27, 1945, the day before her birthday, when she was told that the death sentence would be carried out. Meanwhile, events changed rapidly. British, American, and Russian forces invaded Germany, and Heinrich Himmler ordered the execution of all occupants of Ravensbruck. On May 3 Fritz Suhren, commandant of Ravensbruck, placed Odette in a Mercedes Benz and with a convoy of Gestapo cars drove for two hours and parked in the woods. There, the Germans burned the prison records and had a picnic.

They returned to their cars and drove to an American camp. Suhren turned Odette over to the Americans because she had pretended to be a relative of Winston Churchill. She explained that Suhren was the commandant of Ravensbruck and had him arrested. That night she slept in a car so that she could be outside for the first time since May 25, 1943. After the war she was awarded the George Cross for bravery.

**BIBLIOGRAPHY**

Tickell, Jerrard. *Odette: The Story of a British Agent*. London: Chapman and Hall, 1949; Tickell, Jerrard. "Odette Will Not Confess." In Alfred Perles, ed. *Great True Spy Adventures* (131–39). New York: Arco, 1957; Walters, David William. *Modern Lives*. New York: Collins, 1954 (Juvenile); InWomSup.

# SCHMIDT, KITTY

**(1882–1954)**
**Brothel Owner, Germany**

Kitty Schmidt, who would become a high-priced call girl and amass a great deal of wealth during World War II, was born in Berlin, Germany, in 1882. In 1922 she opened her first brothel in that city and deposited her earnings in a London bank. After the Nazis came to power in 1933, members of her staff helped get the money to London by smuggling it out sewn in specially designed corsets. The Nazis accused her of smuggling two different times, but she managed to stay out of jail. She also used her brothel and money to help Jews escape and in March 1939, decided that she, too, must leave Germany.

On April 4, 1939, she received a visit from Detective Superintendent Eric Kuhn, a member of the brothel surveillance squad. He informed her that Berlin's police chief, Arthur Nebe, planned to place female undercover agents in her brothel. They would steer senior members of the Nazi Party, armed forces, and diplomatic corps to the brothel so that these agents could gather information. In return, he said, Kitty would enjoy an increase in business and the authorities would overlook her lawbreaking activities. She agreed, then tried to escape. The police arrested her at the Dutch border on June 29, 1939, and incarcerated her in the Prinz Albrechtstrasse dungeon where they stripped her of her expensive jewelry, luggage, and mink coat and beat her. She lived on watery coffee, bread, soup and once, a thick stew. She was eventually released and required to report back to SS agent Walter Schellenberg every day at four o'clock in the afternoon. Meanwhile, Schellenberg put Operation

"Salon Kitty" into action on October 18. He turned Schmidt's basement into a monitoring center and trained women agents from Germany, Austria, the Protectorates of Bohemia and Moravia, Poland, and Danzig. The women all had personal problems such as drug use, abortions and illegal activities that were used to keep them in the organization. Twenty of the fifty women they trained were selected to work in Kitty Schmidt's brothel. It became a Central Security Office intelligence center with every conversation overheard, including those of ambassadors, top senior advisors, foreign officers, war office officials, and the foreign minister, Joachim von Ribbentrop. On July 17, 1942, the brothel was bombed, but the explosion only penetrated as far as the first floor. Schmidt was forced out on the street surrounded by her chandeliers, chairs, beds, crockery, and linen. No one was killed or injured and the brothel reopened on July 19. Early in 1943 the Central Security Office closed down Operation "Salon Kitty," and they posted the women agents to other departments. Schmidt disappeared from public view until 1973, when Peter Norden's biography was published.

**BIBLIOGRAPHY**

Norden, Peter. *Madam Kitty*. Trans. J. Maxwell Brownjohn. London: Abelard-Schuman, 1973; BioIn 10.

# SCHOLL, SOPHIE

**(1921–1943)**
**Resistance Fighter, Germany**

Sophie Scholl was born on May 9, 1921, into a family devoted to the arts. Her letters and diaries show her to be idealistic and intuitive. She attended the University of Munich in 1942, where she majored in art and philosophy. As news of Nazi atrocities became more widely known, many students expressed their concern and Scholl exhibited a growing agitation at Germany's situation. The strong morals that Sophie Scholl and her brother Hans had been raised with and the company they kept enabled them to begin a campaign against the Nazi regime. In 1942 Sophie and Hans and a small group of students at the University of Munich, along with their philosophy professor, began an underground resistance movement called the White Rose. Despite the fact that their actions were extremely dangerous, they painted slogans on walls and secretly wrote and distributed leaflets urging the overthrow of the Nazi government and called for an end to the war. The Gestapo quickly traced the movement, arrested and swiftly tried them and beheaded three students on the same day. Sophie Scholl was one of those students. She was twenty-two years old when she went to the guillotine along with her brother Hans, on February 22, 1943. Scholl was remembered as one of the youngest resistance fighters. The last line of one of the White Rose leaflets reads, "We will not be silent. We are your bad conscience. The White Rose will not leave you in peace!"

**BIBLIOGRAPHY**

Jens, Inge, ed. *At the Heart of the White Rose: Letters and Diaries of Hans and Sophie Scholl*. New York: Harper and Row Publishers, 1984; Dumbach, Annette E., and Jud Newborn. *Shattering the German Night*. Boston: Little, Brown and Company, 1986.

## SCHOLTZ-KLINK, GERTRUD

(1902–   )
**Nazi Political Leader, Author, Germany**

Gertrud Scholtz-Klink, a major political leader in the Third Reich, was born in Aelsheim (Baen), Germany, on February 9, 1902. She had little education and after her husband died she was left with six children to support. Two of her six children also died. In 1928 she joined the NSDAP and by 1930 was a leader in the National Socialist Women's Union (NSF). By 1934 she had become the leader of the women's labor service and on February 24, 1934, was named *Reichsführerin* (Female Führer) of the NSF and the German Agency (DFW). In November, she became Reich Women's Führerin and eventually leader of the *Frauenwerk* (a federal organization of women); the Women's League of the Red Cross; the Women's Bureau in the Deutsche Arbeitsfront (German Labor Front); and leader of the Women's Labor Service. In 1950 Scholtz-Klink was identified as a "major offender" and lost her civil rights. In 1978 she wrote *Women in the Third Reich*.

**BIBLIOGRAPHY**

"Dead?" *Time*, March 15, 1948, 39; InWom; BioIn 1, 14; EncTR; GoodHS; Int-DcWB; WhoWNG.

Gertrud Scholtz-Klink. Courtesy of the National Archives.

## SCHULTZ, SIGRID

(1893–1980)
**Founder, Overseas Press Club, United States**

Sigrid Schultz was born in Chicago, Illinois, in 1893, to Herman Schultz and Hedwig Jaskewitz Schultz. Her father was a renowned portrait painter who painted royalty and important government figures worldwide. Sigrid was educated mostly abroad after 1911 at the Lycée Racine in Paris. In 1914 she received a Diplôme de Certificat d'Etudes Supérieures from the Sorbonne in Paris. She witnessed the Kaiser's declaration of the First World War and suffered wartime shortages including a lack of food. (She later wrote that crow was a delicacy.) Her first job was as a secretary, assistant, and interpreter for the mayor of Bagdad while she studied law. In 1919 she became the assistant/secretary to Richard Little of the Chicago *Tribune*. By then she was fluent in German, French, Polish, and Dutch and had become an authority on military strategy and armaments. Finally she was given an assignment of her own—the ex-Kaiser's wedding. After the wedding she reported while under fire in the Tiergarten and also described the corpses in the lobby of the Hotel Adlon and sent dispatches in the midst of Communist riots.

Schultz founded the Overseas Press Club and in 1925 was named chief of the Berlin bureau. As such, she was the official Berlin hostess for the Foreign Press Association and became acquainted with important international figures including future officials of the Third Reich. In 1931 she conducted the first of seven interviews with Adolf Hitler. He told her she would never understand the Nazis because she thought with her head, not her heart. She became openly critical of the Nazis and the propaganda ministry attempted to have her expelled. Undeterred, in 1938 she began a series of weekly broadcasts from Berlin for the Mutual Broadcasting System. In August 1940 shrapnel from a British air raid wounded her in the leg. She managed to drag herself to the studio to broadcast her program, but when she arrived she found that technical difficulties had canceled the airing.

In February 1941 Schultz returned to the United States and suffered a siege of typhus. After she recovered she lectured on tour in the United States. In 1944 she wrote *Germany Will Try It Again*. In the book was a chapter entitled "Women Nazis Are the Worst." Her thesis was that women were more fervent and would educate their children in the Nazi tradition. Schultz eventually began work on an oral history of anti-Semitism commissioned by the American Jewish Committee. She died in Westport, Connecticut, at eighty-seven years old on May 15, 1980.

## BIBLIOGRAPHY

Shave, T. "Week's Work." *Collier's*, November 8, 1947, 8; CurBio 44; ForWC 70; WhoAm 44–45, 74, 76, 80; WhoAmJ 64, 66, 68, 70, 72, 74; InWom; NewYTBS 80; BioIn 12.

# SCHWARZKOPF, ELISABETH

(1915–  )
**Opera Singer, Poland**

Elisabeth Schwarzkopf, one of the foremost sopranos in Germany, was born in Jarotschin, a town in the province of Poznan in West Poland, to Friedrich Schwarzkopf, the director of a high school, and Elisabeth Frohlich Schwarzkopf. The family moved to Berlin and she attended the Berlin High School for music and had private lessons as well. A League of Nations scholarship allowed her to study English in Leicester, England. Easter Day 1938 was the date of her first professional operatic engagement, when she performed at the Deutsches Opernhaus in Charlottenburg on thirty-six hours emergency notice. After her performance the famous Hungarian soprano, Maria Ivogun, took her on as a private pupil.

Unfortunately, a serious incident occurred during this time. Committee members gave the part Schwarzkopf had been promised in the next opera to someone else, and she refused to sing the minor part given her. She put the heel of her shoe through a piece of scenery and was reported to authorities and accused of "sabotage in wartime." For this Schwarzkopf faced possible forced labor in a munitions factory, but her father, who was working on the Eastern front to help identify soldiers killed in conflict and assist their relatives with administrative and funeral arrangements, hurried to Berlin. He and her accompanist-husband, Michael Raucheisen, intervened and convinced authorities she was needed to entertain the troops. The incident was considered forgotten.

In November 1942 Schwarzkopf performed her first *Lieder* recital in Vienna and became a member of the Vienna Opera House. In 1943 she contracted tuberculosis, said to have been caused by the damp air-raid shelters, and retired to recuperate. When she returned to the Vienna State Opera House, she found it had been closed because the auditorium had been bombed. She went into a second temporary retirement. Schwarzkopf sang for army units and at munitions factories, for up to a dozen performances a week. When the Allies advanced, she and her mother escaped to Attersee, near Salzburg. When the Americans arrived, actress Kathe Dorsch rescued her and allowed her to hide in quarters above the chicken run. Eventually she sang for American troops before returning to Vienna in November 1945. However, since she was a German citizen

Elisabeth Schwarzkopf. Courtesy of the Library of Congress.

without a valid passport, the de-Nazification board could not give her a regular contract without being cleared.

Schwarzkopf's career suffered because of allegations that she was a member of the Nazi Party. She once said she was banned by the British, cleared by the French, banned by the Russians, and cleared by the Americans. Regardless, the New York Metropolitan Opera refused to hire her and her records were banned from Israeli radio broadcasts. However, in 1947 she did perform at Covent Garden in London and at the Salzburg Festival. In January 1949 she agreed to a three-month concert tour of Australia. In 1951 she performed at the Bayreuth Festival, at the world premiere of Stravinsky's *The Rake's Progress* in Venice, and at LaScala in Milan. She moved to London and married her second husband, Walter Legge, a recording executive and founder of the London Philharmonic Orchestra. On October 25, 1953, she made her American concert debut at the Town Hall in New York City. She began a tour of United States and eventually made her American operatic debut at the San Francisco Opera Company on September 20, 1955. She continued singing and on October 13, 1964, finally made her debut at the Metropolitan Opera House.

On April 27, 1975, Schwarzkopf's appearance at Carnegie Hall was billed as her farewell U.S. appearance, but she gave her last New York recital on April 27, 1976. On June 10, 1976, she was awarded an honorary doctorate in music from the University of Cambridge in England and that year she and her husband began teaching master classes in vocal interpretation at the Julliard School of Music in New York. She continued to tour and record until 1979, when Legge died and she retired.

## BIBLIOGRAPHY

"Portrait." *Musical America*, September 1955, 4; Ewen, David, ed. *Living Musicians*. New York: Wilson, 1957, 137–38; Milburn, F. "Elisabeth Schwarzkopf—Versatile Artist." *Musical America*, December 15, 1956, 15; WhoAm 78, 80; WhoAmJ 66, 68, 70, 72, 74, 75; WhoWWII 74, 76, 78; InWom; IntDcWB; IntWW 74, 75, 76, 77, 78, 79, 80, 81–82, 83; WhoM 72; Jacobson, R. "Quote . . . Unquote." *Musical America*, September 1963, 44; Brever, G. "Everything In Its Time." *Opera News*, December 19, 1964, 27; Gruen, John. *Close-Up*. New York: Viking Press, 1968; Kolodin, I. "Schwarzkopf in the Sunset Glow." *Saturday Review*, May 21, 1975, 46–47; Christiansen, Rubert. *Prima Donna: A History*. New York: Penguin Books, 1986, 260–164; CurBio; CurBioYrbk 1955; BioIn 3, 4, 5, 6, 7, 8, 10, 11, 12, 13; Baker 78, 84, 92; Who 82, 83, 85, 88, 90, 92, 94; WorAlB; WorAl.

# SENDER, TONI

(1888–1979)
Anti-Nazi Politician, Germany


Toni Sender was born on November 29, 1888, to Moritz Sender, a department store owner, and Marie Dreyfess Sender in Biebrich on the Rhine, later part of Wiesbaden. At thirteen she left home to attend school in Frankfurt and two years later got a job with a real estate firm. At seventeen she was in charge of the mortgage department. Meanwhile, Sender continued to read voraciously and became interested in the labor movement. She joined the Office Worker's Union and was active in political demonstrations. She also became interested in the Socialist movement and in 1910 moved to Paris and joined the Socialist Party. She was appointed vice-chairman of her section and became the permanent delegate to the Federal Council of the Socialist Federation of the Seine. She helped start a women's labor organization, but when World War I broke out in 1914, she returned to Germany. While in Germany Sender helped organize the local National Federation of Proletarian Freethinkers and she was named a delegate to the national convention preparatory to the International Socialist Congress. In 1915 she was in close contact with activists Rosa Luxemburg and Clara Zetkin to organize an International Antiwar Conference. In 1917 the majority Socialists split and she helped organize the Independent Social Democrat Party of Germany. She continued her anti-war efforts and began editing the party newspaper, *Volkstrecht*. Beginning in 1920 she was a member of the Reichstag for thirteen years and editor of the shop council's magazine. In 1921 she became ill with tuberculosis and was sent to Switzerland for a year to recuperate. After her return she made trips to the United States in 1926, 1927, and 1930 to lecture. She also returned to school and became editor of *Frauenwelt, Illustrated Magazine for Women of the Laboring and Middle Classes*.

In 1933, as the Nazis came to power, Sender continued to speak, despite stink bombs and other disruptions. Stones were thrown through her windows and her telephone was tapped. She was slandered in local newspapers and her name was on a list of three people who were to be attacked on March 5. The Nazis distributed leaflets that contained open threats of murder. Finally, she was forced to flee across the Czech border to Belgium. She became an editorial writer on foreign affairs and remained active in the labor movement. In 1934 and 1935 she returned to the United States to lecture and in 1936 emigrated to the United States as an employee of the United States Office of Strategic Services. In the 1950s she was a consultant to the American Federation of Labor and Economic and Social Council of the United Nations and during this time proposed an investigation of forced-labor conditions. She continued to remain active, taking graduate courses, lecturing, researching, and serving as an American correspondent for European news papers until her death in 1979.

**BIBLIOGRAPHY**

*Time*, February 28, 1949, 29; IntWW 1942; Sender, Toni. "Escape from Terror." In Purcell-Lixl, Andreas, ed. *Women of Exile*. New York: Greenwood Press, 1988; Sender, Toni. *The Autobiography of a German Rebel*. New York: Vanguard Press, 1939; WhoAmJ 58, 61; AnnObit of 79; InWom; BioIn 2, 6; CurBio 1950.

# SENDLER, IRENA

(1916– )
**Rescuer, Poland**

Irena Sendler was born in Otwock, Poland, in 1916. When the Germans invaded Warsaw in 1939 she was working in the Social Welfare Department of the Administration of Warsaw. She took advantage of her job to help Jews who were being persecuted and began recruiting trustworthy people to help her issue hundreds of false documents with forged signatures. When the Nazis isolated the Jews in the Warsaw ghetto, she already had 3,000 people identified for help, 90 percent of whom were placed behind the ghetto's walls, which destroyed her efforts. She and her closest collaborator, Irena Schultz, obtained false documents saying they worked for the Special Sanitary Station and this gave them the legal right to enter the ghetto two or three times a day. They established contact with Ewa Rechtman who had organized a secret section of women called the Centos, and who was given the code name "Jolanta." Using their false documents, Sendler and Schultz took food, clothing, medicine, and money into the ghetto. When mass expulsions began in 1942, Sendler was working with the Council for Aid to Jews (RADA Pomocy Zydom), or ZEGOTA. She had a list of addresses in Warsaw where people, particularly children, could stay until they procured "Aryan" documents. They called their efforts the Emergency Care Service. Irena Schultz became the expert at leading children out through underground corridors

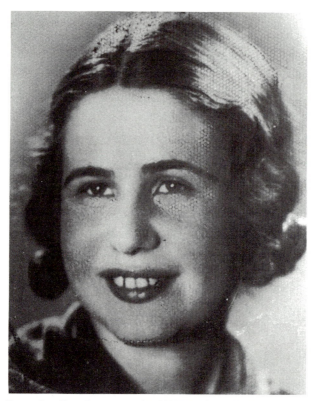

Irena Sendler. Courtesy of USHMM Photo Archives.

of public court buildings and through the train depot. Schultz also organized a special section for medical care.

On October 20, 1943, a secret meeting place in a laundry was discovered. The proprietress was arrested and tortured and gave the Gestapo Sendler's name. Sendler was arrested and put in Pawlak prison, where she was tortured and sentenced to death. On the day she heard her name called for mass execution, she was taken aside for "additional interrogation." Her guard took her outside and set her free on a street corner. Someone on the outside had managed to bribe the Gestapo. The next day her name appeared on the walls of Warsaw for "treason to the Third Reich." She hid in a neighbor's apartment and dared not leave despite the fact that while she was in hiding her mother died.

Her efforts for the Jews continued on a limited basis and in 1965 Yad Vashem recognized her as a "Righteous Among Nations." Sendler made news in March 1997 when *Family Circle* magazine printed the story of twelve-year-old Rebecca Marmor of Manlius, New York, who sent her bat mitzvah money to Sendler, who is now eighty-one years old and living in Warsaw. Marmor picked Irena from a list of rescuers available from the Jewish Foundation for the Righteous that was founded ten years ago to send support checks to nearly 1,300 Christian rescuers in twenty-six countries.

## BIBLIOGRAPHY

Bartoszewski, W., and Z. Lewin, eds. *Righteous Among Nations: How Poles Helped the Jews, 1939–1945.* London: Earls Court Publications Ltd., 1969; "Honoring Those Who Cared." *Family Circle*, March 4, 1997, 13; EncHol.

# SIMAITE, ONA

(1899–1970)
**Rescuer, Lithuania**

Ona Simaite was working as a librarian at Vilna University in Vilna, Lithuania, when the war broke out. Distressed at the treatment of Jews in the community, she began visiting the Vilna ghetto by using the excuse that she needed to collect library books from Jewish students. She accomplished two things: First, she retrieved valuable books given to her by other public institutions such as YIVO (the Yovo Institute for Jewish Research) and private individuals and hid the books in different locations including under the floorboards in her apartment. Second, Simaite negotiated the retrieval of Jewish possessions from non-Jews. When their possessions were returned, the Jews could then trade them to purchase food. She also recruited people to help hide Jews and attempted to rescue a Jewish girl herself. She managed to get the child out of the ghetto and hid her in several places, but the girl was accidentally discovered.

Simaite adopted a ten-year-old Jewish girl by registering her as a relative and used a fictitious address in a bombed-out town. She was arrested in the summer of 1944 and tortured but did not divulge information about her Jewish contacts. Her spine was ruptured during the torture and she would be in pain the rest of her life. She was scheduled for execution, but friends in the academic circles of the university bribed the Gestapo, and she was sentenced to imprisonment in a concentration camp. She was eventually transferred to France and was lib-

Ona Simaite.

erated in 1944. Simaite settled in France and was named a "Righteous Among Nations" by Yad Vashem. She died in 1970.

**BIBLIOGRAPHY**

EncHol.

## SKOBTSOVA, ELIZAVETA (MOTHER MARIA)

**(1891–1945)**
**Resistance Worker, Latvia**

Elizaveta Skobtsova, a Russian Orthodox nun who assisted Jews in France, was born in Riga, Latvia, in 1891 to Juri Pilenko, director of the renowned botanical gardens near Yalta, and Sophia Pilenko. Elizaveta married and divorced, then married again. While pregnant with her second child, she and her husband emigrated to Paris and suffered great financial hardships. When her four-year-old daughter died in 1923, Skobtsova decided to become a nun in the Russian Orthodox Church. In 1932 she took the name of Maria. In 1941 she met I. A. Krivoshein who was organizing aid for prisoners and their dependents in the Compieque detention camp, a hundred kilometers northeast of Paris. She established a committee to organize the preparation and dispatch of food parcels and to raise and distribute funds. The headquarters of the Orthodox Action group in Paris at 77 Rue de Lourmel became a central point of Jewish aid, and Mother Maria became a symbol of resistance to the rising bigotry. When the Germans issued identity cards to Russian émigrés, she scornfully ignored the order, risking arrest by German security police. She said she believed Hitler's Germany to be the contaminator "of all European springs and wells" (Hackell, 108). She called Hitler a "madman, who needs a straitjacket and a cork-lined room so that his bestial wailing would not disturb the world at large" (Hackell, 108). When officials came to put up posters urging Frenchmen to work as volunteers in German factories, she tore them down.

On July 15/16, 1942, a mass arrest of Jews was carried out in Paris. More than 6,900 Jews, 4,051 of them children, were herded into the Vélodrôme d'Hiver sport stadium on the Boulevard de Grenelle, a kilometer from the Lourmel address. The stadium had only one water hydrant and four latrines. Five days later the children were separated from their parents and sent from Drancy, a camp outside Paris, to Auschwitz. Mother Maria gained admission to the stadium and worked among the imprisoned Jews to distribute the minute amount of available food and frantically tried to rescue some of the children before they were deported. She recruited garbage men to help but they were only able to smuggle four children out of the camp. She then returned to 77 Lourmel to help provide Jews with forged documents and to find temporary homes for children whose parents the Nazis had seized on the streets in raids. She aided Jews, émigrés, and one of the first escaped Soviet prisoners of war to flee the city. She made contacts at the local flour mill and obtained bread, flour, groats, and other products for those in hiding. She was interrogated and warned several times to stop her activities but refused to cooperate. Mother Maria was arrested on February 8, 1943, along with thirty-four women at Compiegne Station, and put in a cattle car with 200 other women bound for Ravensbruck concentration camp, where she became prisoner number 19263. Other prisoners would remember her as a cheerful leader who organized groups and led discussions on Russian history and the Orthodox Church. She died of exhaustion on March 31, 1945, days before the liberation and was recognized as a "Righteous Among Nations" by Yad Vashem.

### BIBLIOGRAPHY

Hackel, Sergei. *Pearl of Great Price: The Life of Mother Maria Skobtsova 1891–1945.* Crestwood, N.Y.: St. Vladimir's Seminary Press, 1981; Smith, T. Stratton. *Rebel Nun: The Moving Story of Mother Maria of Paris.* New York: Templegate, 1965; BioIn 7; EncHol.

## SOLF, JOHANNA

(?–1954)
**Rescuer, Germany**

Little is known about the early life of Johanna Solf, an aristocrat who would be known as a member of "Frau Solf's Tea Party." Her father, Dr. Wilhelm Solf of the German Foreign Office, attempted to change the Nazi's treatment of political opponents and Jews. He interceded with Josef Goebbels and attempted to make an appointment with Adolf Hitler. He saved several persecuted professors by getting them minor appointments out of the country. Anti-Nazis began meeting at the Solf house, a casual organization that became known as Solf's Circle. The meetings continued after Wilhelm Solf's death, and the organization then became known as "Frau Solf's Tea Party" by the Gestapo, who had the group under surveillance.

In 1938 the Gestapo interrogated Johanna Solf. They claimed that while Solf lived in Shanghai, until her return to Berlin in 1938, she had been a "political agitator," associating with Jewish friends, expressing anti-Nazi opinions, and refusing to visit the "German corner" where members of the German colony congregated. The Gestapo would later call her in and accuse her of being a "Jew slave." As the nation became more dominated by the Nazis, Solf rebelled in small ways. She carried a shopping bag filled with laundry or vegetables so she would not have to give the "Heil Hitler" salute. She continued to meet at her mother's house to express opinions and listen to foreign radio stations. She helped author and gynecologist Dr. Ferdinand Mainzer escape from Germany.

In the fall of 1940 Solf married Count Hubert Ballestrem, also an opponent of National Socialism who had been fighting the Nazis since before they came to power. She and her mother began obtaining emigration affidavits and visas for Jews and sheltered some people in her mother's home; they helped others find hiding places. They visited apartments marked with Jewish stars forbidden to "Aryans" for lists of needed items and began smuggling Jews into Switzerland. Then, in August 1943, a couple they were hiding was picked up by the Gestapo and gave information against the two women and they were placed under surveillance. In September Solf's mother attended a birthday party given by Fraulein von Thadden, a member of the circle. Johanna did not attend as she was in the hospital. A stranger was present at the event and was described by friends as "of like mind." Frau Solf gave him three letters for the Danish minister in Switzerland. They learned later that the man, a Dr. Reckzeh, was a Gestapo agent, and the Solfs expected to be arrested anytime. November came, however, and no arrest was made. After Johanna Solf's home was bombed during a heavy air raid, she moved in with her mother; soon after, her mother's house was also demolished. Frau Solf moved to Partenkirchen in Bavaria. Johanna remained in Berlin to have surgery, but followed her mother to Bavaria on January 12, 1944. Two hours after her arrival, her mother, her aunt, and her housekeeper were taken to Gestapo headquarters in Munich. They interrogated Frau Solf immediately and the rest were locked in a windowless tower room for three days. The family was told that Frau Solf was in a prison in Berlin. In actuality, the Gestapo were holding her in a cell in a building at Sachsenhausen. In March, guarded by two Gestapo officials in plain clothes, Johanna was taken to Ravensbruck. She found that her mother was in the same prison. She was given sleeping potions then roused for inquisitions that lasted from six to fifteen hours. She was placed on a starvation diet of decaying turnips. In June 1944 members of the circle were put on trial: Frau von Thadden, Fanny von Kurowsky, Irmgard Warden, Dr. Otto Kiep, Consul General in New York, and Legation Counsel Scherpenberg. In the People's Court on July 1 Frau Solf was charged with high treason, sedition, favoring the enemy, and defeatism. The trial lasted from eight o'clock in the morning until eleven o'clock at night.

Frau Solf was withdrawn from the case "for further investigation" and returned to Ravensbruck. Von Thadden was sentenced to death and decapitated with an ax. Dr. Kiep was hanged, Scherpenberg was imprisoned for two years; Fanny von Kurowsky and Irmgard Warden were acquitted. Johanna Solf was to go on trial along with Privy Councellor Kuenzer, Count Bernstorff, the historian, a Dr. Hagen, and Father Friedrich Erxleben, a Jesuit priest. In February 1945 the prison was bombed and the trial was postponed until April 27. On April 23, however, Ballestrem and Solf were discharged from prison. A friend, Dr. Ernst Ludwig Heuss, had persuaded officials to let them go. Frau Solf emigrated to England. A total of seventy-six friends and close acquaintances of the family were killed, many in April 1945, right after Frau Solf and Johanna Solf were discharged. Johanna Solf remained in Berlin until her death in 1954.

### BIBLIOGRAPHY

Boehm, Eric H. *We Survived: Fourteen Histories of the Hidden and Hunted of Nazi Germany*. Santa Barbara, Calif.: ABC-Clio Information Services, 1985; EncTR; *Encyclopedia of German Resistance to the Nazi Movement*. Wolfgang Beuz and Walter H. Pehle, eds. New York: Continuum Publishing, 1997.

## STERNBUCH, RECHA

**1905–1971**
**Rescuer, Belgium**

Recha Sternbuch, called "one of the most influential rescue activists in the Free World" (Kranzler, 194), was born in 1905, daughter of Rabbi Mordechai Rottenberg, chief rabbi of Antwerp prior to World War II. Sternbuch, a brilliant student, delivered lectures on the Torah to students in Antwerp before beginning her rescue activities in 1938, when Germany annexed Austria. She and her husband Isaac Sternbuch became the Swiss representatives of the Va' A D Ha-Hat-Sala (Rescue Committee of Orthodox Rabbis in the United States). Eventually, they had an entire network of border smugglers. The Sternbuchs scrawled their telephone number in way stations along the border and their home became a way station that was open at all hours.

Recha Sternbuch was arrested in 1939 and although threatened with long term incarceration, refused to give the names of her contacts. Authorities released her and she became the head of the Hilfsuerein (sometimes called Hijefs) für Juelische Fluchtlinge in Shanghai (Relief Organization for Jewish Rescue Committee), established to provide aid for rabbis and Yeshiva students stranded in Shanghai.

In 1941 the Sternbuchs changed the name of their organization to the Hilfsuerein für Judische Fluchtlinge im Ausland (Relief Organization for Jewish Refugees Abroad) and began sending food and parcels to concentration camps via the International Red Cross. They also expanded their rescue activities to include Latin America. In addition, Recha made a trip to Italy to obtain 400 Chinese visas. She was in contact with top officials in many countries such as Police Chief Paul Grueninger in St. Gallen, Switzerland. When Swiss policy was rewritten to let refugee couples with small children stay in the country, then changed when officials learned hundreds were using orphans to create "instant" families, Sternbuch pleaded with Papal Nuncio Bernadini to intervene, which he did. The refugees were allowed to stay.

In the spring of 1944 she worked frantically to save the inmates of Vittel detention camp who were about to be deported, despite having South American papers. Along with former Swiss president Dr. Jean-Marie Musy and SS Chief Heinrich Himmler, she negotiated a ransom for the release of the inmates, although the release was never carried out. But because of the Sternbuchs, 1,200 Jews were rescued from Theresienstadt and arrived safely in Switzerland on February 6, 1945. After the war the Sternbuchs extended their efforts to recover Jewish children from non-Jewish homes, orphanages, or convents. Recha Sternbuch died in 1971.

**BIBLIOGRAPHY**

Friedenson, J., and D. Kranzler. *Heroine of Rescue.* New York: Mesorah Publications, Ltd., 1984; Kranzler, D. *The Brother's Blood: The Orthodox Jewish Response during the Holocaust.* New York: Mesorah Publications, Ltd, 1987; EncHol.

# SZENES, HANNAH

**(1921–1944)**
**Resistance Worker, Hungary**

Hannah Szenes, Anglicized as Senesh, was born in Hungary in 1921 to Bela and Catherine Szenes. She was a brilliant student but often suffered from discrimination because she was Jewish. For example, when she was placed in a private Protestant school, she paid triple the tuition that others paid. In September 1937 when she was elected to office in the school literary society, the position was taken away because Jews were not allowed to hold office. In 1939 when it came time for her to attend university, despite the fact that her teachers tried to assure her that she would be one of the few Jews allowed in, she became a Zionist and emigrated to Palestine under the auspices of the Women's International

Hannah Szenes. Beit Hannah Senesh,
courtesy of USHMM Photo Archives.

Zionist Organization. She finally settled at Sdot Yaim. In January 1943,
Szenes decided to return to Hungary although the Germans had taken
over and were persecuting Jews. She wanted to organize emigration for
young people and bring her mother out of Hungary. She heard about a
Palestinian Jewish parachute mission behind the lines in Europe. The
British would provide the training, equipment, and planes; in return, the
parachutists would provide escape routes for Allied airmen who had
been shot down behind the lines or were prisoners of war trying to
escape. On June 12, Szenes enlisted in the British army.

In December 1943, Szenes began training in Tel Aviv. Only two other
women were being trained. One was Haviva Reik who later parachuted
into Czechoslovakia and was captured and executed. The other was
Sarah Braverman who failed to pass the parachute course. In basic training Szenes learned to kill and to parachute. She was taken to Cairo for
intelligence training and taught to fire a Sten gun, a Tommy gun, a
German Schmeisser, and a .45 Colt Automatic. She became part of the

RAF and was commissioned first as a sergeant and later as an officer. In March 1944, much to her disappointment, she learned she would be dropped into Yugoslavia instead of Hungary. On March 13, she arrived in Yugoslavia. Frustrated by the delay in getting into Hungary, she decided to go herself. On May 13, she set out with partisan guides to a border village where she received false papers and was left by herself.

On June 9, 1944, she crossed the border with a small group of people who had previously escaped from Hungary and were going back in. Two of the group approached a small village to find out its name. Suddenly a company of 200 German soldiers appeared in the distance, and she crawled out of the reeds where she was hiding to bury her transmitter and guns. She was arrested and beaten on the palms of her hands and the soles of her feet until she fell unconscious. She refused to divulge the location of the transmitter, but it was found anyway. She was sent to Budapest and on the way there she tried to open the door and jump from the speeding train, but guards pulled her back in. On the train she hid a book of French poems containing the code to the transmitter. In Budapest she was placed in the Horthy Miklos Street Military Prison.

While a prisoner in Budapest Szenes was beaten, her hair was pulled out in fistfuls, and a tooth was knocked out. Her mother was called in and interrogated. She insisted her daughter was in Palestine until guards revealed her daughter was, in fact, in the next room. They had a dramatic reunion, then Catherine Szenes was sent home, only to be arrested a few hours later. She was put in the same prison as her daughter, where matrons sometimes arranged an "accidental" meeting between the two women. Hannah and her mother arranged to spell out words across the courtyard from each other and this method eventually became the main means of communication to all prisoners. She taught her mother Hebrew through this secret code until they moved her next door to her mother in September. On September 11 Hannah was taken away and at the end of the month, Catherine was released. On October 28 Hannah was tried for treason and on November 7 was given one hour to prepare for her death. She was taken into an interior yard inside the prison and strapped to a wooden post. She refused a blindfold and a firing squad executed her.

## BIBLIOGRAPHY

Szenes, Hannah. *Her Life and Diaries*. New York: Schocken Books, 1972; Masters, Anthony. *The Summer That Bled: The Biography of Hannah Senesh*. New York: St.

Martin's Press, 1972; Leven, M. "Of Channah Szenes and Other Secret Agents." *Menorah Journal* 34 (Spring 1946): 122–32; Syrkin, M. "Parachuting from Palestine." *Commentary*, May 1, 1946, 30–38; Moffat, Mary Jane, and O. Painter, eds. *Revelations: Diaries of Women*. New York: Random House, 1974, 67–74; BioIn 1.

# T

## TEN BOOM, CORRIE

(1892–1983)
**Rescuer, Holland**

Corrie ten Boom became involved in the Third Reich at a later age than most. She was born in Amsterdam in 1892 to watchmaker Casper ten Boom and his wife Cor. She had a stable childhood in a deeply religious family. At age twenty she went to Switzerland to learn the watchmaking trade and eventually went to work in her father's shop. When the Germans invaded Holland in 1940, life took a dramatic turn for the forty-eight-year-old woman. Corrie, her sister Betsie, and her father became members of the LD (a national organization that gave assistance to "underdivers"—"people who go underwater") in the town of Haarlem, where the family had moved. The two sisters, dressed in old-fashioned black dresses, ran an underground organization. Corrie was in charge of their organization, which consisted of thirty boys and girls, twenty older men, and ten women. She had a secret room built under the bottom shelf of her closet that could hold approximately eight people. She called it the Angelcrib.

In 1943 as Allied victories became more frequent, the German police in Holland became more vindictive. Another sister, Nollie van Woerden, was arrested for hiding Jews in her home and activities ceased at the ten Boom house until Nollie was released. Then the family returned to pro-

viding rations and travel cards, arranging for transportation, and offering a hiding place to Jews.

On February 28, 1944, a Dutchman arrived at the ten Boom house
asking for money to escape with his wife. The Dutchman was a quisling
secretly working with the Germans. They had ordered him to find out
if Corrie ten Boom was an underground worker. Five minutes after giving him the money, Corrie was arrested along with everyone who entered the shop from that point on, including customers and underground
workers who had seen the ''all clear'' advertisement for Alpine watches
in the window. Six people trapped in one of the hiding rooms were the
only ones to escape three days later out of the total of thirty-five prisoners taken the first day, including all of the ten Boom children and one
grandson. At noon the following day the family was loaded onto a bus
as bystanders wept. They were transported to the seaside town of Schev-
eningen where the Gestapo interrogated them. From there they were
taken to a series of three prisons. Casper ten Boom died ten days later.

Because she was ill, Corrie ten Boom was separated from her family
and placed in solitary confinement until June 6 when she was reunited
with her sister Betsie and placed on a train to Vught, a concentration
camp in Noord-Brabant. The camp was known for having been the
place where seventy-four women were locked in a small cell overnight.
Ten women suffocated, and some of the others went insane. The ten
Boom sisters organized prayer meetings and a club for positive thinking—the Society of Hollanders—in the room where 150 women sat at
tables.

As the Allies advanced on Holland, the Nazis again herded the prisoners into boxcars and took the two ten Boom sisters to Ravensbruck in
Germany. As Corrie, her sister, and the other women marched through
the gates to the prison they were singing.

The two sisters prayed throughout the horrors of Ravensbruck and
did what they could. When 250 of the younger prisoners passed by Corrie's washroom window, she hid in the dark and as each passed, she
whispered a short, religious message. (She learned later that of the 250,
only one had died.) Betsie became ill and was taken to the camp hospital;
Corrie found her body in the hospital washroom with other skeletal
corpses. Four days later, Corrie was suddenly released. On New Year's
Day 1945, she traveled by boxcar back to Holland.

Ten Boom eventually recovered physically from her experiences and
went on to become a world renowned religious author and lecturer. She

wrote *The Hiding Place* (1971); *In My Father's House: The Years Before "The Hiding Place"* (1976); *Tramp for the Lord, Corrie Ten Boom's Prison Letters* (1974); and *Father Ten Boom, God's Man* (1979). She died on April 15, 1983, her ninety-first birthday.

**BIBLIOGRAPHY**

Knaack, Twila. *Special Friends*. New York: Word Books, 1981; obituary in *Christian Century*, May 4, 1983, 424; obituary in *Christians Today*, May 20, 1983, 27; obituary in *Publisher's Weekly*, May 20, 1983, 132; Watson, Jean. *Watchmaker's Daughter: The Life of Corrie Ten Boom for Young People*. New York: Fleming H. Revell, 1982; Rosewell, Pamela. *The Five Silent Years of Corrie ten Boom*. New York: Zondervan, 1986; Straub, Deborah Gillan. *Contemporary Heroes and Heroines, Book II*. New York: Gale Research, 1992, 477–81; Wellman, Sam. *Corrie Ten Boom: Heroine of Haarlem*. New York: Fleming H. Revell, 1973; Snodgrass, Mary Ellen. *Late Achievers: Famous People Who Succeeded Late in Life*. New York: Libraries Unlimited, 1992; White, Kathleen. *Corrie ten Boom*. New York: Bethany House, 1991; Briscoe, Jill. *Paint the Prisons Bright: Corrie ten Boom*. New York: Word, 1991; Carlson, Carole C. *Corrie ten Boom*. Old Tappan, N.J.: Fleming H. Revell Company, 1975.

# THADDEN, ELISABETH VON

**(1890–1944)**
**Underground Worker, Prussia**

Elisabeth von Thadden, executed for her views on National Socialism, was born in Mohrungen, East Prussia (now Morag, Poland), on July 29, 1890. Her father was the chairman of the local council. She opened an Evangelical boarding school at Wieblingen Castle near Heidelberg in 1927, but because of her membership in the Confessing Church, she was forced to leave the school in 1941. She worked with the Red Cross in convalescent homes for soldiers in France, and began entertaining friends with anti-Nazi views in her home. A spy infiltrated the group on September 10, 1943, and turned her in to the Gestapo. They arrested her in January 1944, and took her to Ravensbruck where, on July 1, 1944, the Volk court sentenced her to death on charges of undermining military strength and attempting high treason. She was executed on August 8, 1944, saying "Put an end, O Lord, to all our sufferings."

**BIBLIOGRAPHY**

EncTR; EncHol.

# THOMPSON, DOROTHY

(1893–1961)
**War Correspondent, United States**

Dorothy Thompson, an American war correspondent who was extremely outspoken against the Nazis, was born on July 9, 1893, in Lancaster, New York, to the Rev. Peter Thompson, a Methodist minister, and Margaret Grierson Thompson. She was educated in public schools before obtaining an Associate of Arts degree from Lewis Institute in Chicago. She graduated from Syracuse University in 1914 and worked for the woman suffrage movement in Buffalo, New York, while beginning her career in journalism by selling articles to magazines. On June 19, 1920, she and a friend went to Europe to write. By May 1921 she was a correspondent in Austria for the Philadelphia *Public Ledger*. In 1925 Thompson became the first woman to head a major, overseas American news bureau in Berlin. She published her first book, *The New Russia*, that same year and married author Sinclair Lewis in 1928. She returned to the United States to live with Lewis, and they opened their home to immigrants fleeing to America as Europe escalated toward war.

Thompson was eager to return to work and in 1931 began traveling back and forth between the United States and Europe, writing on the course of the Third Reich and espousing anti-Nazi views in articles such as a portrait of her first Viennese neighbor, a Socialist school teacher who was killed, or a description of Nazi Germany titled "Good-By to Germany." *Cosmopolitan* sent her to interview Adolf Hitler and she wrote a book about the experience titled *I Saw Hitler* (1932) that was one of the first to analyze and present a history of the Nazi movement. In July 1934, Nazi government officials ordered her to leave Berlin because of the interview and her subsequent articles attacking Hitler's anti-Semitic campaigns. She left for Paris and her expulsion made front-page news in America. As a reminder, she kept the framed expulsion order on the wall of her home.

On her return to America, Thompson began a series of lectures on the political climate that proved extremely popular. She also became a columnist for the *Herald Tribune* and *Ladies' Home Journal* and more than three-fifths of her columns were about Hitler. She had a radio program called the *General Electric Hour* that enabled her to continue to attack the Third Reich and challenge isolationists such as Charles Lindbergh. She published *Refugees: Anarchy or Organization* and a *Political Guide* in 1938.

On September 26, 1938, she gave a rousing address at a pro-Czech rally at Madison Square Garden. On February 20, 1939, she attended another rally at the Garden of the German-American Bund where 19,000 supporters of Fritz Kuhn came to hear him denounce "the Jew-loving Roosevelt." Thompson, in attendance as a journalist, was seated in the front row and when a Bund assistant, in hopes of "warming up the audience," began an anti-Semitic tirade, she shocked the audience by laughing. Photographers caught the moment on film and the next day newspapers published a photograph of her being escorted from the auditorium.

Thompson published two more books in 1939—*Once on Christmas* and *Let the Record Speak*—and in 1941 conceived an organization she called "The Ring of Freedom" made up of Allied supporters. She was also honored at a May 6 dinner by the Committee of 1,000 that consisted of Democratic representatives publicly stating their support under the title "Free France," "Free Italy," "Free Poland," etc. She made a tour of England that same year, visiting and describing devastated towns, bomb shelters, and RAF bases. In 1942 she published another anti-German book, *Listen, Hans*.

On October 29, 1944, Thompson delivered one of her most effective speeches, a radio broadcast in which she described the feelings of mothers whose sons were at war. Over half-a-million copies of the speech were mailed out by Franklin Roosevelt's re-election committee afterwards. Ironically, that same day in Italy, a sniper killed Wells Lewis, her beloved stepson.

In April 1945 Thompson flew to Europe to cover the closing days of the war, and described the civilized homes of the SS administrators in the concentration camps—homes filled with classic literature, music, and fine furnishings. After that, her career seemed to ebb. She had divorced Lewis in 1942 and married Maxim Kopf, an artist, the next year. After the war she and her husband suffered financially. Kopf died in July 1958, and Thompson wrote her farewell column for the Bell Syndicate on August 22. She began working on her autobiography and died on January 30, 1961, in Lisbon, Portugal. A large number of her papers was given to the George Arents Research Library at Syracuse University.

## BIBLIOGRAPHY

Burnet, Will, and Charles E. Szatkn. *American Authors Today*. New York: Ginn, 1947; CelR, 1959, 759–60; Drewery, John E. *Post Biographies of Famous Journalists*. New York: Random House, 1928; Fisher, Dorothy Canfield. *American Portraits*. New York: Holt, 1946, 274–77; Muir, Jane. *Famous Modern American Writers*. New York: Dodd, 1959; "Dorothy Thompson." *New Yorker*, April 20, 1940, 24; "Dorothy Thompson." *New Yorker*, April 27, 1940, 24; Rogers, Agnes. *Women Are Here to Stay*. New York: Harper and Row, 1936; Holtz, William, ed. *Dorothy Thompson and Rose Wilder: Forty Years of Friendship Letters, 1920–1960*. Columbia: University of Missouri Press, 1991; Kurth, Peter. *American Cassandra: The Life of Dorothy Thompson*. Boston: Little, Brown and Company, 1990; Sanders, Marion K. *Dorothy Thompson: A Legend in Her Time*. Boston: Houghton-Mifflin Company, 1973; "Columnist Bows Out." *Newsweek*, September 1, 1958, 39–40; obituary in CurBio, March 1961, 45; obituary in *Newsweek*, February 13, 1961, 68; obituary in *Publisher's Weekly*, February 13, 1961, 130; obituary in *Time*, February 10, 1961, 66; obituary in CurBioYrbk, 1961, 19; 1962, 453; Sheean, Vincent. *Dorothy and Red*. New York: Houghton-Mifflin, 1963; Sheean, Vincent. "Dorothy and Red." *Harper's*, October 1963, 123–72; "Teller of Tales." *Time*, November 15, 1963, 119; Broun, H. "Right People." In *Faces of Five Decades*. New York: Simon and Schuster, 1964, 259–69; Jakes, John. *Great Women Reporters*. New York: Putnam, 1969; Ross, Ishbel. *Ladies of the Press*. New York: Arno Press, 1974, 360–66; Fang, Irving E. *Those Radio Commentators*. Ames: Iowa State University Press, 1977, 131–49; CurBio 40; WomPO 76, 78; AnnObit of 79; DcAmB 7; NotAW: Mod; WhE&EA; WhoAmJ 58, 61; AmAu&B; AmWomWr; BioIn 1, 2, 4, 5, 6, 7, 9, 10, 11, 12; ConAu 89; EncAB; EncTR; GoodHS; InWom; IntDcWB; OxAm; REn; REnAL; TwCA 991–2; WebAB; WhAm 4; WorAu.

# TILLION, GERMAINE MARIE ROSINE

(1907–   )
**Resistance Leader, France**

Germaine Tillion, head of a resistance network in France, was born in Allegre, France, on May 30, 1907, to Jacques Tillion and Emilie Cussac Tillion. She received an M.A. from the University of Paris as well as diplomas from the Practical School of Advanced Studies, the National School of Living Oriental Languages, and the School of the Louvre. From 1939 to 1940, she conducted ethnographic missions in the Aurès, Algeria.

When World War II broke out, Tillion became the head of the Musée de L'Homme chapter of the French Resistance and her mother became an active participant. She and her mother were arrested on August 13, 1942, and Germaine's case was marked "NN", which stood for *Nacht und Nebel* (Night and Fog), the designation for prisoners who were considered dangerous to the Third Reich and slated to disappear. Tillion found out later that she had been identified by the priest and vicar of LaVarenne, Father Robert Alesch, who infiltrated the network and was paid to identify members of the Resistance. Tillion was taken to Santé prison, then Fresnes, where she was interrogated and accused of seven acts of treason, five of which carried the death penalty, including harboring English agents. In April 1943 she managed to see her mother when their two doors opened simultaneously. They both waved and tried to smile; the guard wept. They were deported on October 21, 1943, and eventually Tillion was transferred to Ravensbruck. On February 3, 1944, her mother also arrived at Ravensbruck but was moved to Romainville in August and eventually killed. Meanwhile, in January 1944, Tillion was able to take secret photographs of children with gangrenous legs and hide them in a pocket; she also managed to take notes in codes disguised as recipes on high echelon SS people in the camp.

Tillion was liberated on April 23, 1945, due to the efforts and negotiations of the Swedish Red Cross and Count Folke Bernadotte. She helped investigate German war crimes and Soviet concentration camps from 1945 to 1954 and wrote a book called *Ravensbruck* (1946). She received the Commander of Legion of Honor, the croix de guerre, and the Rosette of Resistance. She eventually became an anthropology professor at the Sorbonne from 1954 to 1962; in addition, she was an investigator in Algeria (1954–62) and educational director at the Professional School of Advanced Studies in 1957. Tillion wrote *Algeria: The Realities* (1957) and *France and Algeria: Contemporary Enemies* (1960). From 1964 to 1965 she participated in the National Science Research Center mission among the Tuaregs in the Sahara Desert and Moors in North Africa.

## BIBLIOGRAPHY

Tillion, Germaine. "Night and Fog." In *Women in the Resistance and in the Holocaust: The Voices of Eyewitnesses*. Vera Laska, ed. (198–207). Westport, Conn.: Greenwood Press, 1983; IntDcWB; WhoF 79; ConAu 104; WhoWor 74.

# V

## VOORT, HANNA VAN DER

(?–?)
**Rescuer, Holland**

Hanna van der Voort grew up in Tienray, in the Limburg province in Holland. When the war started, she dedicated herself to saving Jewish children and eventually found hiding places for 123 children. She worked with an underground organization who identified the children for her. It was her job to find temporary and permanent homes and transfer the children when they were in danger of being discovered. The Germans eventually discovered van der Voort's activities and arrested and tortured her. The torture she endured resulted in lifelong health problems. Van der Voort and the man she worked closely with, Nico Dohmen, were named as "Righteous Among Nations" by Yad Vashem.

**BIBLIOGRAPHY**

EncHol.

# W

## WAGNER, WINIFRED

(1897–1980)
**Friend of Hitler, Great Britain**

The woman who would one day become one of Adolf Hitler's closest friends was born in Hastings, England, to an actress mother and engineer father on June 23, 1897. Both parents died before she was two years old, and a Danish grandfather was asked to take the young child. Overwhelmed by the responsibility, he committed suicide and Wagner was then placed in an orphanage. When she was ten years old a distant relative living in Germany, Karl Klindworth, adopted her. Klindworth, a pianist-conductor and former student of Franz Liszt, took her to see Siegfried Wagner, son of Richard Wagner, at the Bayreuth Festival in 1914. A year later she was married to the forty-five-year-old composer, one of the wealthiest and most sought-after bachelors in Germany. Wagner immediately became involved in the Festival, aiding her husband as secretary and attending to all the business details of his concert tours.

In 1920 or 1921, Winifred Wagner met a young man named Adolf Hitler and was soon espousing his philosophies, attending rallies, and waving swastikas on street corners. Her husband first viewed the relationship with humor, but later admitted he could not control her growing involvement in the Nazi movement. Wagner's daughter would later say that her mother, while not one of the original seven Hitler supporters, was certainly "among the first few hundred." When Hitler and his aides were jailed in 1923, Wagner collected food and clothes for the families of the prisoners and sent typewriter paper, carbon paper, pencils, pens, ink, and erasers to Hitler that he used to write *Mein Kampf.* After his release in 1925, Wagner brought Hitler and his aides to the Wagner family home, Wahnfried, and hid them overnight, since Hitler's life was still in danger. Afterwards, she continued to meet him in out-of-the-way places.

Siegfried Wagner died on August 4, 1930, and the next morning Winifred was in his office taking over the family affairs. Siegfried's associates were outraged and the Bayreuth mayor and city fathers urged her to turn the family home over to the city for a Wagner museum; they had already found another home for her. With major moral and financial support from Hitler, who was an avid Wagner aficionado and attended the Festival every year, Wagner stayed and turned the Bayreuth Festival into one of the most important events on the Nazi social calendar. Throughout the Third Reich, Wahnfried was one of Hitler's favorite retreats. He was even involved in the Wagner family life and often intervened in the upbringing of the Wagner children. It was rumored that Hitler and Wagner would marry.

After the war, Wagner was forbidden to run the Bayreuth Festival and little was heard of her until 1972 when she was interviewed by J. Barkas for *Opera News.* In subsequent interviews she was unrepentant about her relationship with Hitler and said "she would never regret meeting him." She died in Uberlingen on March 5, 1980.

**BIBLIOGRAPHY**

Barkas, J. "Frau Wagner, Interview." *Opera News*, July 1972, 20–21; Donner, W. "Winifred Wahnfried Wagner." *Encounter*, December 1975, 33–37; obituary in NewYT, March 6, 1980, D19; obituary in NewYTBS, March 11, 1980, 467; obituary in *Newsweek*, March 17, 1980, 86; NewYTBS 80; EncTR.

# WIGMAN, MARY

**(1886–1973)**
**Dancer, Choreographer, Germany**

Mary Wigman, a German dancer and choreographer who was a leader of the pioneer modern-dance movement during the Third Reich, was born in Hanover, Germany, on November 13, 1886. She was educated in

Hanover and in boarding schools in England and Switzerland. On a visit to Amsterdam she saw a dance performance by students of Emile Jacques Dalcroze, the originator of a system of musical instruction, and decided she wanted to become a dancer. Despite her parents' objections, she joined Rudolf von Laban as a teacher at his school in Ascona, Switzerland, in 1913, and became his assistant at his new school in Zurich in 1914. In 1918 she suffered a physical breakdown and convalesced at a Swiss mountain retreat. The next year she presented her first dance compositions, which critics called "ridiculous," "idiotic," and "mad." Other of her presentations were more successful, and by 1920 she was dancing at the Dresden Opera and had founded the Mary Wigman Central Institute. In 1924 she toured Central Europe; 1928 was her first appearance in London. In 1929 German government authorities honored her nationally and recognized her locally on the tenth anniversary of her first professional appearance. She toured the United States in 1930, 1931, and 1932 and was said to have had a lasting influence on American dance.

In 1931 her assistant, Hanya Holm, established the Mary Wigman School in New York, but Communist leaders approached Holm and wanted her to make a statement that although Wigman was living in Germany, she had nothing to do with Hitler. Holm refused, saying it would cost Wigman her life. The New York school was boycotted and protestors threw stones through the windows. The two women decided that changing the name of the school would be safer and it became the Hanya Holm school. Wigman's school in Germany continued to run undisturbed until 1936 when Wigman performed the opening dance at the Olympics. (Holm later excused Wigman's decision saying it was "an Olympic thing, not a German thing.") Meanwhile, the Nazis labeled Wigman's art "degenerate," "decadent," and "un-German" and they took control of the German school. In 1942, she moved to Leipzig where her sister Elizabeth ran a branch of the Mary Wigman School. The city was bombed, but Wigman refused to go to the bomb shelter saying the experience inspired her. She worked under Soviet occupation and lived among ruins, destitute and in ill health. She continued to dance and choreograph, however, and in 1949 she opened a new school in West Berlin, subsidized by the West Berlin Senate.

After the war Wigman was invited to lecture at Connecticut College for Women, but could not get a visa. Her last public performance was in 1953, however, she continued to choreograph for dance and opera productions in Germany. She was awarded the Great Cross of the Order of Merit of the German Federal Republic in 1957 and in 1958 the New

York Public Library gave a special exhibition of Wigman memorabilia. She was awarded the Art Prize of Berlin in 1952, the Schiller Prize of Mannheim in 1954, and the Dance Prize of the Association of German Critics in 1961. In 1966 the city government of West Berlin honored her in a special celebration on her eightieth birthday. She died on September 19, 1973.

## BIBLIOGRAPHY

*Christian Science Monitor*, May 12, 1964, 4; *Dance Magazine*, November 1966, 40; *New York Herald Tribune*, November 11, 1956, 5; "Wigman at 80: Still an Influence." NewYT, November 13, 1966, 28; Hurok, S. *Impresario*. New York: Random House, 1946; Hurok, Solomon. *Hurok Presents*. New York: Hermitage, 1953; Maynard, Olga. *American Modern Dancers*. New York: Little, Brown, 1965; Manning, Susan. *Ecstasy and the Dance: Feminism and Nationalism in the Dances of Mary Wigman*. Berkeley: University of California Press, 1993; obituary in *Time*, October 1973, 79; Siegal, M. B. "Mary Wigman 1886–1973: A Tribute." *Dance Magazine*, November 1973, 80–81; Wigman, Mary. *Mary Wigman Book: Her Writings*. Ed. and trans. Walter Sorrell. Middletown, Conn.: Wesleyan University Press, 1975: Odom, M. "Mary Wigman: The Early Years, 1913–1925." *Drama Review*, December 1980, 81–92; CurBio 1969, 41–44; CurBioYrBK 1969, 448–51; NewYTBS 73; AnnObit of 79; InWom; BioIn 1, 3, 4, 7, 8, 10, 12; IntDcWB.

# WUNDERLICH, FRIEDA

**(1884–1965)**
**Professor, Germany**

Frieda Wunderlich, who was one of ten German professors and the only woman brought to the United States by the New School for Social Research in 1933, was born in Berlin, Germany, in 1884. In the pre-Nazi era, she was a member of the Prussian State Parliament and of the Berlin City Council. She served as a judge of the German Supreme Court for Social Welfare and was editor of the *Soziale Praxis (Social Research)*, an anti-Nazi political weekly, from 1923 to 1933. After her arrival in the United States, Wunderlich was a member of the graduate faculty of political and social research known as "the University in Exile" and was unanimously elected dean for the academic year 1939–40 of the graduate faculty. She was a professor of economics, labor, and sociology until 1954. She wrote several books on labor and social problems including *Farm Labor in Germany Until 1945* (1961). She also became a member of the International Labor Office Committee on

Frieda Wunderlich. Courtesy of USHMM Photo Archives.

Woman's Work. She died on December 29, 1965, in East Orange, New Jersey, at the age of 76.

**BIBLIOGRAPHY**

Obituary in NewYT, December 31, 1965, 21.

# Y

## YAMAIKA, ZOFIA

(1925–1943)
**Resistance Worker, Poland**

Zofia Yamaika, a Polish resistance heroine, was born in 1925 to a prominent Hassidic family in Warsaw, Poland. In high school she belonged to the radical student club Spartacus whose members, among other activities, printed anti-Fascist posters and leaflets in a toy printing shop. In the fall of 1940 Yamaika and her family were forced to live in the Warsaw ghetto. Zofia managed to finish high school in the ghetto even though education was illegal. She went to a special training course in leadership for fighters and after the course became the leader of a children's group in her father's House Committee. (House committees oversaw the needs of a single courtyard. The Yamaikas' committee was one of 2,000 in the ghetto.) Her main goal was to provide food for her group. When Kazik Denbiak infiltrated the ghetto to recruit members for the first anti-Fascist partisan detachment, Yamaika volunteered. The group gave additional training courses in weaponry and nursing skills and prepared to escape to the forest. Her main concern was leaving her parents, who would be punished for her escape under the law of collective responsibility initiated by the Germans. On July 22, 1942, however, the Germans began deporting thousands of Jews to the concentration camps and Yamaika's parents were among those deported.

In August 1942, Yamaika escaped to the forest after she was smuggled into the cemetery work area outside the ghetto. From there she and other partisan members were taken to the small town of Biala-Podliaski where they were to wait for a courier to take them into the forest. Unfortunately, the Germans started deportations in the Biala-Podliaski ghetto as well, and Yamaika was among those rounded up. She was placed in a cattle car bound for Treblinka. When the German guards opened the doors of the car to remove the bodies of those who had died en route, she pretended to be dead. She was left along the roadside and rescued by a local peasant who hid her until she could make her way back to Biala-Podliaski.

When the courier did not arrive, Yamaika was forced to return to Warsaw. She wandered the streets without possessions, money, or papers until she met a Polish underground worker named Eva Pewinskia who had volunteered her home as a way station for partisans headed for the forest. Pewinskia obtained forged Aryan papers for Yamaika and got her a job working for an illegal printing press publishing the *Guardist*, an underground newspaper. On September 28 and 29, 1942, the Gestapo discovered the press, raided it, and arrested Yamaika.

She was taken to Pawiak prison as was Eva Pewinskia. They released her in December 1942 and Yamaika was destitute, left again to wander the streets of Warsaw. Fortunately, she recognized an underground worker who arranged for Yamaika to reach the forest. Before this could happen, a German policeman stopped her and demanded to see her papers. She had none and was forced to shoot him. She and her Polish guide then made several more attacks on police and were armed when they reached the partisan group Levi on December 30, 1942.

During Yamaika's time in the forest, she was assigned to reconnaissance because of her knowledge of German. She also acted as a liaison between the partisan units and the General Staff. On January 12, 1943, the group captured the town of Gowarczow in the region of Konsk, Radom district. The partisans cut telephone wires and destroyed the police station and German headquarters. Among the records they obtained during the raid was a list of Nazi agents and collaborators. Yamaika was then given the task of killing the spies and agents. She was decorated for bravery by the General Staff. On February 9, 1943, 300 Germans entered the forest bent on retaliation for the Gowarczow raid. The partisans, who numbered only around fifty, retreated further into the forest; Yamaika volunteered to stay behind with a machine gun to cover the retreat. She was killed in the battle and was buried by the Germans, but later the partisans dug up her body and gave her a military funeral. In April 1963, the Polish government posthumously awarded her the Virtuti Military medal, one of the highest military awards possible.

### BIBLIOGRAPHY

Mark, Esther. "Zofia Yamaika." In *They Fought Back: The Story of the Jewish Resistance in Nazi Europe*. Ed. Yuri Such. New York: Crown Publishers, 1967.

# Z

## ZASSENHAUS, HILTGUNT

**(1916–  )**
**Resistance Worker, Germany**

Hiltgunt Zassenhaus, called the German Angel for her wartime activities that helped keep track of some 1,200 prisoners, was born in 1916 to Julius Zassenhaus, a former Lutheran minister and headmaster of a girls' high school, and his wife Margaret, active in reforming the Social Democratic Party. In 1933, while attending high school in Hamburg, Hiltgunt was assigned to write a report on Adolf Hitler's speech at the Victoria sports ground. She labeled him "psychotic" and when the students in her school were ordered to give the "Heil, Hitler" salute, she refused. She was given twenty-four hours to obey.

The next day, the entire class, as well as the teachers and principal, were watching to see what Zassenhaus would do. Her arm jerked and went through a nearby window and she was taken to the hospital. After that, when it came time to offer the salute, she was ignored. The day Hitler came to power in 1933, the Zassenhaus home was covered with swastikas and eventually Julius was dismissed as headmaster. The family's books and writings were burned. When the police arrived at the house to arrest Julius, they found him too ill with Parkinson's disease to move. They required Hiltgunt to join the German Girls' League, but she let her membership lapse after only one week. Her mother, meanwhile, was working to help Jews to escape.

In 1938 Zassenhaus graduated from the University of Hamburg with a degree in Scandinavian languages and became the only female interpreter in Danish and Norwegian at the court of Hamburg. On September 1, 1939, she was given the job of censoring Scandinavian mail. While working in this capacity, she began smuggling messages on scraps of paper, including toilet paper, from the Jews in the ghettos. She smuggled letters out of the censor's office and made sure they were sent to relatives in Scandinavia. When hundreds of prisoners from Norway were placed in Fuhlsbuttel prison, officials gave her the job of censoring their mail and supervising their visits by the pastor of Hamburg's Norwegian Seaman's Mission. On her first visit, authorities brought in twenty starving prisoners wearing rags and wooden shoes. By the end of the war, Zassenhaus had contact with over 1,200 Scandinavian prisoners. She committed all the details of their families to memory, and despite orders to the contrary, she gave them news from home and passed them photographs and messages. She brought in bread, vitamins, medicine, pencils, paper, and chewing tobacco. The Gestapo interrogated her three times.

On July 24, 1943, Operation Gomorrah, an Allied air offensive from July 24 to August 3, 1943, designed to destroy the German port of Hamburg, began and Zassenhaus's workload increased dramatically as political prisoners poured into Germany. She fashioned a card index system to keep track of information on more than 1,000 prisoners. When prisoners were transferred to other prisons, she tracked them with her file. On August 22, 1944, her youngest brother, Willfried, was killed in Russia and the Zassenhaus home was filled with strangers who had been bombed out of their homes. They illegally listened to the BBC from London with blankets over their heads to hide the sounds of the radio and baked bread with flour purchased on the black market with the family silver. As the war progressed, however, even these activities were curtailed, and Zassenhaus went to Dresden to try to find thirty of her original prisoners who were missing. She was there when the Allies bombed Dresden in February 1945. After a short stay in Berlin, she returned to Dresden to find that the Swedish Red Cross had negotiated with Heinrich Himmler to release the Danish and Norwegian prisoners. Her files became vital in tracking down the prisoners so that they could be released.

After the war Zassenhaus helped look for war orphans. She appealed to the former prisoners for help and they responded with food and clothing. In 1947 she was the first German after the war to be invited to Norway and Denmark, where she was regarded as a national heroine.

She studied medicine in Copenhagen, and in 1952, she and her mother emigrated to the United States where she practiced medicine. In 1979, producers invited her to return to Europe to relive her wartime experiences for British television.

## BIBLIOGRAPHY

Sim, Kevin. *Women at War: Five Heroines Who Defied the Nazis and Survived*. New York: William Morrow and Company, 1982; ConAu 49; BioIn 10, 11; WhoAm 80, 82.

# ZIMETBAUM, MALA

(1920 or 1922–1944)
Camp Prisoner, Auschwitz Escapee, Poland

Mala Zimetbaum, said to be the first woman to escape from Auschwitz, was born in Brzesko, Poland, in 1920 or 1922. Her family moved to Belgium in the 1930s and settled in Antwerp where Zimetbaum joined Hanoar Hatzioni, a Zionist youth group. When her father became blind, she was forced to leave school and go to work to help support the family. In September 1942, Zimetbaum was caught, arrested, and sent to Auschwitz.

Zimetbaum spoke several languages and so was given the prestigious job of interpreter in the camp. She was also used as a "runner," which enabled her to move from one part of the camp to another. She used her position to help families contact each other and carry messages and medicine. One of her jobs was to assign prisoners released from the hospital to work detail. She assigned the weak to light work and warned patients of coming gas-chamber selections, thus saving many lives. She also became part of the camp underground.

In 1944 Zimetbaum met a young Polish prisoner named Adek Galinski who, as a mechanic, was allowed into the women's section of the prison to fix machines. He was in contact with the underground, which was going to help him escape so he could warn the world of the atrocities at Auschwitz. He included Zimetbaum in his plans and the two managed to break out on June 24, 1944.

When guards counted the prisoners that evening and found prisoner no. 19880 missing, Zimetbaum became a camp heroine. It was believed that Galinski and Zimetbaum reached the Slovak border before being arrested and returned to Auschwitz two weeks later. The Nazis tortured them to find out how they had escaped and who had helped them. Nevertheless, they divulged no information. They were sentenced to hanging as a lesson to the other prisoners, but both managed to avert that fate by attempting to commit suicide. Zimetbaum had a concealed razor blade and cut an artery on her wrist. When the SS tried to stop her, she slapped his face with her damaged hand. The guard screamed at her and struck her with his revolver. He dragged her into the hospital and her wrist was bound so that she would not bleed to death. Then she was beaten. Her mouth was taped shut so that she could not shout encouragement to the horrified women looking on. She was taken to the crematorium. The Antwerp government honored her as a "symbol of solidarity" by placing a plaque on the Zimetbaum house.

## BIBLIOGRAPHY

Weisblum, Giza. "The Escape and Death of the 'Runner' Mala Zimetbaum." In *They Fought Back: The Story of the Jewish Resistance in Nazi Europe*. Ed. Yuri Suhl (182–84). New York: Crown Publishers, 1967; EncHol.

# APPENDIX A: ROLES

## ARTISTS

Kollwitz, Kathe, Germany

Salomon, Charlotte, Germany

## ATHLETES

Mauermayer, Gisela, Germany

Mayer, Helene, Germany

## AUTHORS

Dodd, Martha Stern, United States

Frank, Anne, Germany

Huch, Ricarda Octavia, Germany

Keun, Irmgard, Germany

Kolmar, Gertrud, Germany

Ludendorff, Mathilde, Germany

Mann, Erika, Germany

Neurath, Wendelgard von, Germany

Reiss, Johanna Deleeuw, Holland

Scholtz-Klink, Gertrud, Germany

## HIDDEN CHILDREN

Frank, Anne, Germany

Reiss, Johanna Deleeuw, Holland

Reitsch, Hanna, Germany

## JOURNALISTS AND COMMUNICATIONS

Anderson, Jane, United States

Drexel, Constance, Germany

Gillars, Mildred Elizabeth, United States

Higgins, Marguerite, United States

Schultz, Sigrid, United States

Thompson, Dorothy, United States

## NAZIS AND NAZI SYMPATHIZERS

Anderson, Jane, United States

Braun, Eva, Germany

Braunsteiner, Hermine, Germany

Gillars, Mildred Elizabeth, United States

Goebbels, Magda, Germany

Goering, Emmy, Germany

Grese, Irma, Germany

Mauermayer, Gisela, Germany

Reitsch, Hanna, Germany

Scholtz-Klink, Gertrud, Germany

Wagner, Winifred, Great Britain

## PERFORMING ARTISTS

Bergner, Elisabeth, Film Actress, Germany

Dagover, Lil, Actress, Germany

Dietrich, Marlene, Actress, Germany

Fenelon, Fania, Musician, France

Giehse, Therese, Actress, Germany

Goering, Emmy, Actress, Germany

Leider, Frida, Opera Singer, Germany

Lubin, Germaine, Opera Singer, France

Mann, Erika, Actress, Writer, Germany

Porten, Henny, Silent Film Star, Germany

Riefenstahl, Leni, Film Director, Actress, Germany

Schwarzkopf, Elisabeth, Opera Singer, Poland

Wigman, Mary, Dancer, Choreographer, Germany

## POLITICAL PRISONERS

Gluck, Gemma La Guardia, United States

Harnack, Mildred Fish, United States

Thadden, Elisabeth von, Prussia

## POLITICIANS AND POLITICAL DISSIDENTS

Dodd, Martha Stern, United States

Scholtz-Klink, Gertrud, Germany

Sender, Toni, Germany

## RESCUERS

Abegg, Elisabeth, Germany

Fleischmann, Gisi, Slovakia

Getter, Matylda, Poland

Kluger, Ruth, USSR

Kutorgiené-Buivydaite, Elena, Lithuania

Nevejean, Yvonne, Belgium

Sendler, Irena, Poland

Simaite, Ona, Lithuania

Solf, Johanna, Germany

Sternbuch, Recha, Belgium

Ten Boom, Corrie, Holland

Voort, Hanna, van der, Holland

## RESISTANCE (WORKERS AND FIGHTERS)

Arendt, Hannah, Germany

Astrup, Helen, Norway

Bar Oni, Bryna, Poland

Bohec, Jeanne, France

Capponi, Carla, Italy

Chevrillon, Claire, France

Cohn, Marianne, Germany

Delbo, Charlotte, France

Fiocca, Nancy, France

Fleischmann, Gisi, Slovakia

Fourcade, Marie-Madeleine, France

Friang, Elizabeth, France

Gloeden, Elizabeth Charlotte Lilo, Germany

Huch, Ricarda Octavia, Germany

Jongh, Andrée de, Belgium

Kasprzak, Ida Dobrzanska, Poland

Kleist, Ruth von, Prussia

Komorowski, Irena Kwiatkowska, Poland

Korczak-Marla, Rozka, Poland

Lund, Sigrid Hellieson, Norway

Mansbacher, Herta, Germany

Meed, Vladka Petel, Poland

Musu, Marisa, Italy

Neurath, Irmagard von, Germany

Neurath, Wendelgard von, Germany

Rutkiewicz, Maria Kamieniecka, Poland

Sansom, Odette Bailly, France

Scholl, Sophie, Germany

Skobtsova, Elizaveta (Mother Maria), Latvia

Thadden, Elizabeth von, Prussia

Tillion, Germaine Marie Rosine, France

Yamaika, Zofia, Poland

Zassenhaus, Hiltgunt, Germany

Zimetbaum, Mala, Poland

## SCIENTISTS, MATHEMATICIANS, PHYSICIANS, AND PROFESSORS

Adelsberger, Lucie, Physician, Germany

Brewda, Alina, Physician, Poland

Hautval, Adelaide, Physician, Lithuania

Mansbacher, Herta, Schoolteacher, Germany

Meitner, Lise, Scientist, Germany

Noether, Emmy, Mathematician, Germany

Perl, Gisela, Physician, Hungary

Wunderlich, Frieda, Professor, Germany

## SOLDIERS

Capponi, Carla, Italy

Kuntsevitch, Sophia, Ukraine

Mikhaylova, Katyusha, USSR

Musu, Marisa, Italy

Popova, Nadya, USSR

Reik, Haviva, Slovakia

Reitsch, Hanna, Germany

Szenes, Hannah, Hungary

Richard, Marthe, French Spy, France

## SPIES

Bancroft, Mary, Swiss Spy, United States

Brousse, Amy Elizabeth, British Spy, United States

Butler, Josephine, British Spy, Great Britain

Carré, Mathilde-Lily, French Spy, France

Granville, Christine, British Spy, Poland

Katona, Edita, French Spy, Austria

Massing, Hede, Soviet Spy, United States

## UNDERGROUND (FIGHTERS AND WORKERS)

Adamowicz, Irena, Poland

Brewda, Alina, Poland

Cook, Ida W., Great Britain

Cook, Louise, Great Britain

Dönhoff, Marion, Germany

Draenger, Tova, Poland

Glazer, Gesja, Lithuania

Grossman, Haika, Poland

Komorowski, Irena Kwiatkowska, Poland

Lubetkin, Zivia, Poland

Thadden, Elisabeth von, Prussia

# APPENDIX B:
## COUNTRY OF ORIGIN

**AUSTRIA**

Hohenlohe-Waldenburg, Stefanie Richter, Deportee

Katona, Edita, French Spy

**BELGIUM**

Jongh, Andrée de, Resistance Fighter

Nevejean, Yvonne, Rescuer

Sternbuch, Recha, Rescuer

**FRANCE**

Bohec, Jeanne, Resistance Fighter

Carré, Mathilde-Lily, French Spy

Chevrillon, Claire, Resistance Fighter

Delbo, Charlotte, Resistance Fighter

Fenelon, Fania, Musician, Camp Prisoner

Fiocca, Nancy, Resistance Fighter

Fourcade, Marie-Madeleine, Resistance Fighter

Friang, Elizabeth, Resistance Fighter

Lubin, Germaine, Opera Singer

Richard, Marthe, French Spy

Sansom, Odette Bailly, Resistance Fighter

Tillion, Germaine Marie Rosine, Resistance Leader

**GERMANY**

Abegg, Elisabeth, Rescuer

Adelsberger, Lucie, Physician, Camp Prisoner

Arendt, Hannah, Zionist, Resistance Worker

Bergner, Elisabeth, Actress

Braun, Eva, Mistress of Hitler

Braunsteiner, Hermine, Nazi Camp Guard

Cohn, Marianne, Resistance Fighter

Dagover, Lil, Actress

Dietrich, Marlene, Actress, Anti-Nazi

Dönhoff, Marion, Underground Worker

Drexel, Constance, Journalist

Frank, Anne, Author, Hidden Child

Giehse, Therese, Actress

Gloeden, Elizabeth Charlotte Lilo, Resistance Worker

Goebbels, Magda, Socialite, Nazi

Goering, Emmy, Actress, Nazi

Grese, Irma, Prison Camp Warden, Nazi

Huch, Ricarda Octavia, Author, Resistance Worker

Keun, Irmgard, Author

Kollwitz, Kathe, Artist

Kolmar, Gertrud, Poet

Leider, Frida, Opera Singer

Ludendorff, Mathilde, Author

Mann, Erika, Actress, Writer, Anti-Nazi

Mansbacher, Herta, Schoolteacher, Resister

Mauermayer, Gisela, Athlete, Nazi

Mayer, Helene, Athlete

Meitner, Lise, Scientist

Neurath, Irmagard von, Resistance Worker

Neurath, Wendelgard von, Author, Resistance Worker

Noether, Emmy, Mathematician, Anti-Nazi

Porten, Henny, Silent Film Star

Reitsch, Hanna, Pilot, Nazi

Riefenstahl, Leni, Film Director, Actress

Salomon, Charlotte, Artist

Schmidt, Kitty, Brothel Owner

Scholl, Sophie, Resistance Fighter

Scholtz-Klink, Gertrud, Nazi Political Leader, Author

Sender, Toni, Anti-Nazi Politician

Solf, Johanna, Rescuer

Wigman, Mary, Dancer, Choreographer

Wunderlich, Frieda, Professor

Zassenhaus, Hiltgunt, Resistance Worker

## GREAT BRITAIN

Butler, Josephine, British Spy

Cook, Ida W., Underground Worker

Cook, Louise, Underground Worker

Wagner, Winifred, Friend of Hitler

## HOLLAND

Reiss, Johanna DeLeeuw, Hidden Child, Author

Ten Boom, Corrie, Rescuer

Voort, Hanna van der, Rescuer

## HUNGARY

Perl, Gisela, Physician, Camp Prisoner

Szenes, Hannah, Resistance Worker

## ITALY

Capponi, Carla, Partisan Fighter

Musu, Marisa, Partisan Fighter

## LATVIA

Skobtsova, Elizaveta (Mother Maria), Resistance Worker

## LITHUANIA

Glazer, Gesja, Underground Fighter

Hautval, Adelaide, Physician, Camp Prisoner

Kutorgiené-Buivydaite, Elena, Rescuer

Simaite, Ona, Rescuer

## NORWAY

Astrup, Helen, Resistance Fighter

Lund, Sigrid Hellieson, Resistance Worker

## POLAND

Adamowicz, Irena, Underground Leader

Bar Oni, Bryna, Partisan Fighter

Brewda, Alina, Physician, Camp Prisoner

Draenger, Tova, Underground Leader

Getter, Matylda, Rescuer

Granville, Christine, British Spy

Grossman, Haika, Underground Worker

Kasprzak, Ida Dobrzanska, Resistance Fighter

Komorowski, Irena Kwiatkowska, Resistance Fighter

Korczak-Marla, Rozka, Zionist, Resistance Fighter

Lubetkin, Zivia, Underground Leader

Meed, Vladka Petel, Resistance Fighter

Rutkiewicz, Maria Kamieniecka, Resistance Fighter

Schwarzkopf, Elisabeth, Opera Singer

Sendler, Irena, Rescuer

Yamaika, Zofia, Resistance

Zimetbaum, Mala, Camp Prisoner, Auschwitz Escapee

## PRUSSIA

Kleist, Ruth von, Resistance Fighter

Thadden, Elisabeth von, Underground Worker

## SLOVAKIA

Fleischmann, Gisi, Resistance Fighter, Rescuer

Reik, Haviva, Risistance Fighter

## UKRAINE

Kuntsevitch, Sophia, Soldier

## UNITED STATES

Anderson, Jane, Nazi Propagandist

Bancroft, Mary, Swiss Spy

Brousse, Amy Elizabeth, British Spy

Dodd, Martha Stern, Author, Political Dissident

Gillars, Mildred Elizabeth, Nazi Propagandist

Gluck, Gemma La Guardia, Political Prisoner

Harnack, Mildred Fish, Political Prisoner

Massing, Hede, Soviet Spy

Schultz, Sigrid, Founder, Overseas Press Club

Thompson, Dorothy, War Correspondent

## USSR

Kluger, Ruth, Rescuer

Mikhaylova, Katyusha, Soldier

Popova, Nadya, Combat Pilot

# BIBLIOGRAPHY

Adams, William D. *Dictionary of English Literature.* New York: Gordon Press, 1972.

*American Literary Yearbook.* New York: Gordon Press, 1976.

*American Men and Women of Science.* New York: R. R. Bowker, 1989– .

*The Annual Obituary.* Detroit: St. James Press, 1979– .

*Author's and Writer's Who's Who.* London: Burke's Peerage, Limited, 1934–1971.

Bailey, Martha J. *American Women in Science: A Biographical Dictionary.* Denver, Colo.: ABC-CLIO, 1994.

Baker, Theodore. *Baker's Biographical Dictionary of Musicians.* New York: Schirmer Books, 1978– .

Bartoszewski, Władysłau, and Zofia Lewinowna, eds. *Righteous Among Nations: How Poles Helped the Jews, 1939–1945.* London: Earlscourt Publications, 1969.

Baudet, Marcel et al. *Historical Encyclopedia of World War II.* New York: Facts on File, 1980.

Bauer, Eddy, and James Lawton Collins. *The Marshall Cavendish Illustrated Encyclopedia of World War II.* New York: Marshall Cavendish Corporation, 1972.

Bawden, Liz-Anne. *The Oxford Companion to Film.* New York: Oxford University Press, 1976.

Baxter, Richard. *Women of the Gestapo.* London: Quality Press, 1943.

Beard, Mary R. *Woman as Force in History.* New York: Macmillan Company, 1946.

Bent, William Rose. *The Reader's Encyclopedia.* New York: Thomas Y. Crowell, 1965.

Berenbaum, Michael. *The World Must Know: The History of the Holocaust as told in the United States Holocaust Memorial Museum.* Boston: Little, Brown and Company, 1993.

*Bio-Base: A Periodic Cumulative Master Index on Microfiche to Sketches Found in About 500 Current and Historical Biographical Dictionaries.* Detroit: Gale Research, 1984.

*Biographical Index.* New York: W. W. Wilson, 1937–1996.

Bluel, Hans Peter. *Sex and Society in Nazi Germany.* New York: Bantam Books, 1974.

Boehm, Eric H. *We Survived: Fourteen Histories of the Hidden and Hunted of Nazi Germany.* Santa Barbara, Calif.: ABC-CLIO Information Series, 1985.

Bridenthal, Renate, et al., eds. *When Biology Became Destiny: Women in Weimar and Nazi Germany.* New York: Monthly Review Press, 1984.

Browning, Hilda. *Women Under Fascism and Communism.* London: Lawrence Publishing, 1934.

Burke, W. J., and Will D. Howe. *American Authors and Books, 1640 to the Present Day.* 3rd rev. ed., revision by Irvin Weiss. New York: Crown, 1962.

Campbell, D'Ann. *Women at War with America: Private Lives in a Patriotic Era.* Cambridge: Harvard University Press, 1984.

Center for the American Woman and Politics Staff. *Women in Public Office: A Biographical Directory and Statistical Analysis.* Metuchen, N.J.: Scarecrow Press, 1978.

*Concise Dictionary of American Biography.* New York: Scribner's, 1980.

*Concise Dictionary of American Literary Biography.* Detroit: Gale Research Company, 1987.

*Contemporary Authors: A Bio-bibliographical Guide to Current Authors and Their Work.* Vol. 1–. Detroit: Gale Research, 1962– .

*Current Biography.* New York: Wilson Co., 1940– .

*Current Biography Yearbook.* New York: H. W. Wilson Co., 1955– .

Dean, Basil. *The Theatre at War.* London: Harrap, 1956.

Derek, Theodore. *Women and Children Under the Swastika.* New York: Universum Press, 1936.

*Dictionary of American Biography.* New York: Scribner's, 1928–1937.

*Dictionary of Scientific Biography.* New York: Charles Scribner's Sons, 1974.

Domandi, Agnes Korner, ed. *Modern German Literature: A Library of Literary Criticism.* New York: Frederick Ungar Publishing Co., 1972.

Dornermann, Louise. *German Women Under Fascism: A Brief Survey of*

*Women up to the Present Day*. London: Allies Inside Germany, 1943.

Duke, Maurice, Jackson R. Bryer, and M. Thomas Inge. *American Women Writers: Bibliographical Essays*. Westport, Conn.: Greenwood Press, 1983.

Durand-Wever, Anne-Marie. "Marriage Advice Stations or Married and Engaged Couples." *Family* 2 (May 1930): 85–87.

*Encyclopedia of Espionage*. London: New England Library, 1972.

Evans, Richard J. "Feminism and Female Emancipation in Germany, 1870–1945: Sources, Methods and Problems of Research." In *Central European History*, 48, 1976 Supplement, pp. 123–75.

Ewen, David, ed. *Musicians Since 1900: Performers in Concert and Opera*. New York: H. W. Wilson Company, 1978.

*Foremost Women in Communications*. New York: Foremost American Publishing, 1970.

*Foremost Women of the Twentieth Century*. New York: Melrose, 1987.

Free German League of Culture in Great Britan, ed. *Women Under the Swastika*. London: Free German League, 1942.

Gallagher, Hugh Gregory. *By Trust Betrayed: Patients, Physicians, and the License to Kill in the Third Reich*. New York: Henry Holt and Company, 1990.

Garland, Henry, and Mary Garland. *The Oxford Companion to German Literature*. Oxford: Oxford University Press, 1986.

Garrety, John Arthur, ed. *Encyclopedia of American Biography*. New York: Harper and Row, 1974.

Gill, Anton. *An Honorable Defeat: A History of German Resistance to Hitler, 1933–1945*. New York: Henry Holt and Company, 1994.

Grunberger, Richard. *The Twelve Year Reich: A Social History of Nazi Germany, 1933–1945*. New York: Ballantine Books, 1971.

Guirdham, Arthur. *Revolt Against Pity: An Indictment of the Nazi Martyrdom of Women*. London: Drowther, 1943.

Gutman, Israel, ed. *Encyclopedia of the Holocaust*. New York: Macmillan, 1990.

Halliwell, Leslie. *The Filmgoer's Companion*. New York: Hill and Wang, 1974.

Hamilton, A. "Woman's Place in Germany." *Survey Graphic* 23 (January 1931): 26–29.

Hardin, James, ed. *German Fiction Writers, 1914–1945*. Detroit: Gale Research Company, 1987.

Harris, Ann Sutherland, and Linda Nochlin. *Women Artists, 1550–1950*. Los Angeles: Los Angeles County Museum of Art, 1976.

Hart, James David. *The Oxford Companion to American Literature*. New York: Oxford University Press, 1983.

Herrman, Elizabeth Ruschi, and Edna Huttenmaier Spitz. *German Women Writers of the Twentieth Century*. Oxford: Pergamon, 1978.

Herzberg, Max J. *The Reader's Encyclopedia of American Literature*. New York: Thomas Y. Crowell, 1962.

Hoehn, Matthew, ed. *Catholic Authors*. Newark, N.J.: St. Mary's Abbey, 1947.

Hoes, Durwood. *American Women, 1935–1940: A Composite Biographical Dictionary*. Detroit: Gale Research, 1981.

Huston, Nancy. "The Matrix of War: Mothers and Heroes." In *The Female Body in Western Culture*, ed. Susan Rubin Suleiman (119–39). Cambridge: Harvard University Press, 1986.

*International Author's and Writer's Who's Who*. Cambridge, England: International Biographical Centre, 1918– .

*International Who's Who in Music*. New York: Current Literature Publishing Company, 1918– .

Ireland, Norma O., ed. *Index to Women of the Modern World, from Ancient to Modern Times*. Metuchen, N.J.: Scarecrow Press, 1970.

James, Edward T., et al., eds. *Notable American Women, 1607–1950*. Cambridge, Mass.: The Belknap Press of Harvard University, 1971.

Jetter, Hal. *Women of the Swastika*. Evanston, Ill.: Regency Books, 1963.

Johnson, Rossiter. *The Twentieth Century Biographical Dictionary of Notable Americans*. New York: Gordon Press, 1972.

Keegan, John, ed. *Who Was Who in World War II*. New York: Thomas Y. Crowell Publishing, 1978.

Kirk, Tim. *The Longman Companion to Nazi Germany*. London: Longman, 1995.

Kirkpatrick, Clifford. *Nazi Germany: Its Women and Family Life*. Indianapolis, Ind.: Bobbs-Merrill Company, 1978.

Klein, Ernst. "Women and National Socialism." *Fortnightly* 157 (1975): 285–92.

Klein, Leonard S., ed. *Encyclopedia of World Literature in the Twentieth Century*. New York: Frederick Ungar Publishing Co., 1982.

Kline, Rayna. "Partisans, Godmothers, Bicyclists and Other Terrorists: Women in the French Revolution and Under Vichy." *Proceedings of the Western Society for French History*, no. 5. Niwot: University of Colorado Press, 1977.

Kolinsky, Eva. *Women in Contemporary Germany*. Providence, R.I.: Berg Publishers Limited, 1989.

Koontz, Claudia. *Mothers in the Fatherland: Women, the Family and Nazi Politics*. New York: St. Martin's Press, 1986.

Kunitz, Stanley J., and Howard Haycraft. *Twentieth-Century Authors: A Biographical Dictionary of Modern Literature, Complete in One Volume with 1850 Biographies and 1700 Portraits*. New York: Wilson, 1942.

Lane, Hana Umlauf, ed. *The World Almanac Book of Who's Who*. New York: World Almanac Publications, 1980.

Laska, Vera, ed. *Women in the Resistance and in the Holocaust: The Voices of Eyewitnesses*. Westport, Conn.: Greenwood Press, 1983.

Lauretis, Teresa de. *Feminist Studies-Critical Studies*. Bloomington: Indiana University Press, 1986.

Leek, Ann. "Women in the Third Reich." *Female Studies* 9 (1975): 200–201.

Leuner, H. D. *When Compassion Was a Crime: Germany's Silent Heroes, 1933–1945*. London: Oswald Wolff, 1966.

*McGraw-Hill Encyclopedia of World Biography*. New York: McGraw-Hill, 1975.

Mainiero, Lina, ed. *American Women Writers: A Critical Reference Guide from Colonial Times to the Present*. 5 vols. New York: Ungar, 1979–1994.

Mason, Timothy W. "Women in Germany, 1925–1940: Family, Welfare and Work." *History Workshop* 1 (Spring 1976).

Nakamura, Joyce, ed. *Something about the Author*. Detroit: Gale Research, 1987.

*New Encyclopedia of the Opera*. New York: Hill and Wang, 1971.

*New York Times Biographical Service: A Compilation of Current Biographical Information of General Interest, 1970–*. New York: Times Books, 1970.

Owings, Alison. *Frauen: German Women Recall the Third Reich*. Camden, N.J.: Rutgers University Press, 1993.

Pascal, Francine. *Who's Who*. New York: Bantam, 1990.

Pauweis, Jacques R. *Women, Nazis and Universities: Female University Students in the Third Reich, 1933–1945*. Westport, Conn.: Greenwood Press, 1984.

Phayer, Michael. *Protestant and Catholic Women in Nazi Germany*. Detroit, Mich.: Wayne State University Press, 1990.

Preston, Wheeler. *American Biographies*. Reprint of the 1940 edition. Detroit, Mich.: Omnigraphics, 1975.

Purcell-Lixl, Andreas, ed. *Women of Exile: German-Jewish Autobiographies Since 1933*. Westport, Conn.: Greenwood Press, 1988.

Raven, Susan. *Women of Achievement: Thirty-five Centuries of History*. New York: Harmony Books, 1981.

Richardson, Kenneth, and R. Clive Willis, eds. *Twentieth Century Writing: A Reader's Guide to Contemporary Literature*. London: Newnes, 1969.

Romig, Walter, ed. *The Book of Catholic Authors*. Stratford, N.H.: Ayer Publishers, 1977.

Rose, Ramona M. *Position and Treatment of Women in Nazi Germany*. Vancouver, British Columbia: Tantalus Research, 1984.

Rossiter, Margaret L. *Women in the Resistance*. New York: Praeger, 1986.

Rupp, Lella J. "Mother of the Volk: The Image of Women in Nazi Ideology." *Signs* 3 (Winter 1977): 363–79.

Sachse, Carola. *Industrial Housewives: Women's Social Work in the Factories of Nazi Germany.* New York: Institute for Research in History and the Haworth Press, 1987.

Saywell, Shelley. *Women in War.* New York: Viking Penguin, 1985.

Scher, Helen, and Christine Romero, eds. *German Women Writers in the Twentieth Century.* Oxford: Berg Publishers, 1988.

Schwartz, Paula. "Redefining Resistance: Women's Activism in Wartime France." In *Behind the Lines: Gender and the Two World Wars*, edited by Margaret Randolph Higonnet et al. (141–54). New Haven, Conn.: Yale University Press, 1987.

Sicherman, Barbara, et al., eds. *Notable American Women: The Modern Period.* Cambridge, Mass.: The Belknap Press of Harvard University Press, 1980.

Siegel, Mary-Ellen. *Her Way: A Guide to Biographies of Women for Young People.* Chicago: American Library Association, 1984.

Sim, Kevin. *Women at War: Five Heroines Who Defied the Nazis and Survived.* New York: William Morrow and Company, 1982.

Snyder, Louis L. *Encyclopedia of the Third Reich.* New York: McGraw-Hill, 1976.

Stephenson, Jill. *The Nazi Organization of Women.* London: Croom Helm, 1981.

Suhl, Yuri, ed. *They Fought Back: The Story of the Jewish Resistance in Nazi Europe.* New York: Crown Publishers, 1967.

Syrkin, M. *Blessed Is the Match: The Story of Jewish Resistance.* Philadelphia: JPS, 1977.

Thomas, Katharine. *Women in Nazi Germany.* London: Victor Gollancz Ltd., 1943.

Thomas, Theodore N. *Women Against Hitler.* Westport, Conn.: Praeger, 1995.

Troger, Annemarie. "German Women's Memories of World War II." In *Behind the Lines: Gender and the Two World Wars*, edited by Margaret Randolph Higonnet et al. (285–99). New Haven, Conn.: Yale University Press, 1987.

Uglow, Jennifer. *The International Dictionary of Women's Biography.* New York: Continuum, 1982.

Vinson, James, ed. *American Writers Since 1900.* Chicago: St. James Press, 1983.

Wakeman, John, and Stanley J. Kunitz. *World Authors.* New York: H. W. Wilson, 1975.

Walker, Malvi. *Chronological Encyclopedia of Adolf Hitler and the Third Reich.* New York: Carlton Press, 1978.

Ward, Robert E. *A Bio-Bibliography of German-American Writers, 1670–1970*. White Plains, N.Y.: Kraus International Publications, 1985.

*Webster's American Biographies*. New York: Merriam-Webster, 1975.

Weitz, Margaret Collins. "As I Was Then: Women in the French Resistance." *Contemporary French Civilization* 10 (1986): 145–52.

Weitz, Margaret Collins. Introduction to *Outwitting the Gestapo*, by Lucie Aubrac. Lincoln: University of Nebraska Press, 1993.

Weitz, Margaret Collins. *Sisters in the Resistance: How Women Fought to Free France*. New York: John J. Wiley & Sons, 1955.

*Who's Who: An Annual Biographical Dictionary*. New York: St. Martin's Press, 1982– .

*Who's Who in America*. Chicago: Marquis Who's Who, 1934– .

*Who's Who in American Art, 1991–1992*. New York: R. R. Bowker, 1991.

*Who's Who in American Jewry, 1955–* . Los Angeles, Calif.: Standard Who's Who, 1980.

*Who's Who in France*. Paris: J. Lafitte, 1953/54.

*Who's Who in Government*. Chicago: Marquis Who's Who, 1972/73–1977.

*Who's Who in Hollywood*. New York: Facts on File, 1992.

*Who's Who in the Theatre*. Detroit: Gale Research, 1912–1981.

*Who's Who in the World, 1971/72*. Chicago: Marquis Who's Who, 1971/72.

*Who's Who in World Jewry, 1955–* . New York: Pitman, 1955– .

*Who's Who of American Women*. New Providence, N.J.: Marquis Who's Who, 1958–1995.

Wistrich, Robert S. *Who's Who in Nazi Germany*. New York: Macmillan Publishing Co., 1982; rev. ed., London: Routledge, 1995.

Woodsmall, R. "Women in the New Germany." *Forum*, no. 93 (May 1935): 279–303.

World Almanac Editors. *The Good Housekeeping Woman's Almanac*. New York: Newspaper Enterprise Association, 1977.

World Almanac Editors. *The World Almanac Biographical Dictionary*. New York: World Almanac, 1990.

Zentener, Christian, and Friedemann Bedurftig, eds. *Encyclopedia of the Third Reich*. New York: MacMillan, 1991.

Zophy, Angela Howard, and Frances M. Kavenik. *Handbook of American Women's History*. New York: Garland, 1990.

# INDEX

## About the Authors

SHAARON COSNER is an independent scholar specializing in women's studies. She is the coauthor of *American Women Historians, 1700s–1900s: A Biographical Dictionary* (Greenwood, 1977) and the author of several other books. She teaches at Corona del Sol High School in Tempe, Arizona.

VICTORIA COSNER is a graduate student at the University of Maryland, specializing in nineteenth-century material culture and mourning practices. She works at a museum in Washington, D.C., as a Supervisory Museum Technician.